GETTING THROUGH

weekly thoughts & prayers
from a pandemic

Ruth Crofton

McKnight
& Bishop

About The Publisher

McKnight & Bishop are always on the lookout for new authors and ideas for new books. If you write or if you have an idea for a book, please email:

info@mcknightbishop.com

Some things we love are undiscovered authors, open-source software, Creative Commons, crowd-funding, Amazon/Kindle, faith, social networking, laughter and new ideas.

Visit us at **www.mcknightbishop.com**

ISBN 978-1-905691-71-5

A CIP catalogue record for this book is available from the British Library.

First published in 2021 by McKnight & Bishop Inspire, an imprint of:

McKnight & Bishop Ltd
26 Walworth Crescent, Darlington DL3 0TX
http://www.mcknightbishop.com | info@mcknightbishop.com

This book has been typeset in Garamond, Malgun Gothic and Gill Sans MT.

Printed and bound in Great Britain by United Print, London WC2B 5AH

Introduction

When the first Lockdown was announced and churches had to suspend services, I had been preparing to join with the celebrations of the fifth anniversary of the redevelopment of the building of Jesmond United Reformed Church, Newcastle-upon-Tyne. This had been a huge and successful half-million pound work and my own part had been as Chair of the Development Group so it was a project dear to me. Disappointed not to be able to celebrate, the idea came to me of producing two simple A4 posters for the church noticeboard, rejoicing at the anniversary, and also producing a page of thoughts and a prayer for distribution to church members so that the occasion was still noted with joy and thanksgiving.

This led to a further thought, because I found the thought of people seeing church doors firmly closed week by week a painful one. What if I produced posters each week, on a relevant topic? Then passers-by would see something new each week and know that, though the building was closed, the church had not gone away! I felt that continuing to share thoughts and prayer on the same theme and using the same images as the posters would be a way of maintaining connection between church members and even perhaps with the community and might just help people at this hard time.

There was a mixed response: mostly enthusiasm, but some nay-sayers claimed that the posters would be a waste of time as no-one was out and about. In fact, the reverse was true: people were out walking rather than scurrying by in cars and had time to stop and look and read (they were spotted doing so!) and I tried always to ensure that the material could interest non-Christians too.

At first, I was sending the material to contacts in three churches, and they distributed them by email, also printing copies for those with no internet access. Ere long interest grew, and my email list of churches and individuals grew longer and longer, many people passing them on to others who in turn passed them on, so that the project quickly took on a life of its own. Something I had imagined lasting a few weeks continued for sixty –

3

they were produced each week from 29th March 2020 to 23rd May 2021 - and reached an amazing number of people. Just how many I don't know but, to my certain knowledge, they travelled as far as South Africa!

Then voices were raised in several quarters suggesting that they should be collected together and printed in book form. It was argued that they were not only a resource (several had already been used and adapted in worship) but were also almost a history of the Lockdown which sadly continues, as I write.

A goodly number of people had contacted me to say that these Thoughts and Prayers had greatly helped them to get through Lockdowns and the restrictions laid upon us, hence the title, "Getting Through" seemed apt.

This all began as a response to the Lockdown, and I have retained the original dates as a matter of interest, but the reflections in this book are not restricted to it. Some connect to the Church's year, and some to the natural world. Others begin with a current aspect of the Lockdown, then branch out into a wider consideration of the themes. For example, "Being Masked" begins with the wearing of masks because of the virus, but goes on to the way in which we all wear 'masks' that can disguise our real selves. Thus they are adaptable to many situations, and I think it's significant that from the outset I named the file folder on my computer "Thoughts and Prayers in Crisis" rather than, "during Lockdown."

And so I offer them to you to enjoy and to reflect upon, whether you read straight through, alone or with others, or dip in and out. Please feel free to use and adapt them as you will, the only caveat being that if you are using them in public, please acknowledge the source. Where specific copyright is noted, permission will be needed to use those items.

Ruth Crofton, June 2021

Acknowledgements and Thanks

I have been much encouraged by those who have received these thoughts and sent them on over a wide area, and for the positive feed-back received. I have been especially encouraged to publish by the Elders of Waddington Street United Reformed Church, Durham and Jesmond United Reformed Church, Newcastle-upon-Tyne who, unasked, volunteered to sponsor the work.

My warmest thanks to Helen Gordon for so willingly bringing her imagination and artistic gifts to the production of the new art-work for this book. Thank you, too, to Catherine Richardson, who gave me permission to take any images from her website produced for the finals of her fine arts degree. The photographs of Jesmond United Reformed Church are by Ian Whaley, to whom I am grateful for the rich collection of images he sent me. I believe that this work would be the poorer without all this significant input. The rest of the photographs are my own.

Thanks are also due to Alison Shiel for her careful proof-reading, such an important task.

Last but not least, a big thank you to Mark McKnight of McKnight and Bishop for all his work undertaken in the publishing of this work.

It is generally agreed that the Pandemic and Lockdowns have acerbated mental health issues. All profits from the sale of this book will be given to the Waddington Street Resource Centre, Durham, which this year celebrates its fortieth anniversary as a significant local resource for those with long-term mental health issues.

Happy Anniversary
Jesmond United Reformed Church

Five years ago, on Sunday 29th March, a service of celebration marked the completion of the redevelopment of this church.

"But will God indeed dwell upon earth? Even heaven and the highest heaven cannot contain you, much less this house that I have built!"
(1 Kings 8: 27, Solomon's prayer for the Temple in Jerusalem)

Like Solomon, we know that our buildings are not the only places we can find God, but they are nevertheless significant. The building whose redevelopment we celebrated five years ago has stood as a sign of the eternal presence of God through good times and through hard, and of his love shown to us in Jesus. Sign too, that meeting there are followers of

Jesus, who try to live the life of peace and justice to which he calls us. This matters when people are distressed, as today.

Presently scattered among many homes, we continue to pray in thanksgiving for past, present and future blessings for the world, knowing that God indeed is not restricted to one place, but that his Spirit is with us, a constant guide and comfort.

Pause for a moment and reflect on the hard times you've lived through and the good around us now: the blessings of today.

Loving, living God, we bring to you the past,
with its joys and sorrows, its ease and hardships.
We bring to you the present - our confused moments and our
future hopes . . .
and pray healing of body and mind . . . and may your Spirit
continue to guide us
into understanding and truth. May those who, at this troubled
time
seek release from anxiety, find true peace of mind and joy.
We ask it in Jesus' name.   Amen

Palm Sunday

Jesus said, "If these were silent, the stones would shout out."

(Luke 19: 40)

Luke 19: 28-40

Riding a donkey and not the noble horse a powerful man would use, the people saw that Jesus was someone who was with them, understood them and all their problems; yet at the same time they saw him as the man who could bring them freedom from the oppression they were under. No wonder they cheered and lined the pathway in front of him!

By contrast, Jesus himself knew he was riding towards his own death, when he would face and carry the massive burden of the sin of the world, but through his death and his rising again would bring life - real, full life – to the whole earth. I love that image of the stones themselves rejoicing. the burdened earth itself reaching for freedom, something very relevant to our present age as we become more aware of our misuse of God's creation.

Jesus brings life still, for us, today, as we long for the time when the people and the very earth itself will rejoice together in peace.

Hosanna! Blessed is he who comes in the name of the Lord!

Pause for a moment and reflect on all that is good and precious and hopeful for you, no matter how small.

Loving, living God, thank you that even when things seem bad, you are with us. When we are confused, you understand. When we are happy, you are happy with us.
We bring to you all who are burdened down by a sense of their own guilt; by a sense of their own unworthiness. Those burdened by illness or loss. Those who suffer for speaking out for the poor and dispossessed. All who long to be free.

By your Holy Spirit, bring healing and peace to a hurting world, we pray, and help us all find joy in the present moment. Thank you, Lord, that we are loved so much that Jesus was willing to give his life for us and for all the earth.
Amen

Thoughts for Holy Week and Easter 2020

9th April: Maundy Thursday
Matthew 26: 17-56

Normally, on Maundy Thursday, we would be holding a Communion Service with reflections on Jesus' prayer and arrest in the Garden of Gethsemane.

The sharing of bread and wine and fellowship one with the other, is central to our life together as a worshipping community, but, prevented as we are from meeting at the present time, a suggestion for Thursday.

First, at some time in the day, read the above passage and try to imagine yourself into it. Then, in the evening, as you prepare your own evening meal, remember that others are doing so too, and have done so for years past, in palaces and hovels, and in the upper room. You are part of all that, whether you are with family or alone. Hold that thought as you eat.

Then after your meal, make time for a psalm, as did Jesus and his disciples. You might like to use your favourite or perhaps one of the following, all of which offer comfort: Psalm 121, 130, 131, 139.

If you have a garden, you might like to just go out and be aware of the world around you, or if not, look out of a window. The sky is pretty great! And wait, with Christ.

Lord Jesus, your disciples were tired and fell asleep, were afraid and ran away. We are so often just like that, yet we want to be different. We want to stay awake and pray with you. Want to be brave and hold on. Yet we fail, so often, but today we are here, and will wait, for we love you, Lord, as you love us more than we can imagine.
Amen

10th April: Good Friday

Matthew 26: 57- 27: 55

I am reading Hilary Mantel's *The Mirror and the Light*, and it has reminded me that in Tudor times, if you'd done something that made the authorities accuse you of treason, it was important to have someone powerful to speak up for you. Not to get you off the charge, but to plead that you had the quicker death of decapitation rather than the lingering agony of hanging, drawing and quartering.

Jesus had no-one to speak up for him; quite the contrary, and the mode of execution chosen was the most humiliating possible. Crucifixion was reserved for the poorest, the slave, to frighten everyone. Acutely painful, yes, and we tend to concentrate on that, but it was also made as humiliating as possible. I suspect I'm not alone in not wanting to imagine how that depth of humiliation felt. Yet Jesus went through it, and even offered forgiveness.

And as he died, the curtain that guarded the Holy of Holies in the Temple ripped open. From what was truly a depth of humiliation and pain, the love of God streamed forth.

Loving Lord God, our Father, we cannot imagine the depth of Jesus' love and of his suffering. We cannot imagine the depth of suffering that is the lot of many in the world today. Yet we know that you hold all in your great love, and that, through Jesus' death, that love flows freely to all.
Help us, by your Spirit, to respond to your love with our love and to pray and act always for the bringing of your kingdom, for which Jesus gave his life. In his name we pray.
Amen

11th April: Easter Eve
Matthew 27: 57-66

Including this day might come as a bit of a surprise to you, for we tend to ignore it - well, nothing happened! Perhaps that's the point. It's a time of quiet, of peace. Not usually, of course, because we normally (that word again!) spend it rushing around shopping or travelling or cleaning or a million and one other busynesses. Yet surely it is a day for peace.

One of my favourite pictures is this, 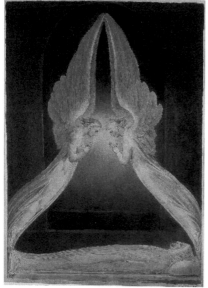 Christ in the Tomb Guarded by Angels, by William Blake. The angels' faces are calm, their wings rising to meet and create a safe, protected space for Jesus' body after all the struggle and suffering.

That combination of peace and protection seems to me so important at this stage in the Easter story, and in our lives now, when everything seems confused and confusing.

Spend time with the picture. Relax. Be at peace.

12th April: Easter Day
Matthew 28: 1-15

"The strife is o'er, the battle done!"

This may be a very odd Easter Day, without physically coming together in worship, but it isn't the first and it won't be the last abnormal Easter Day!

The first Easter found the authorities and the disciples themselves confused. The women who had faithfully gone to the tomb were blessed by seeing the risen Jesus, but Matthew is strangely quiet over how their news was received! It took time to begin to realise the truth of what had happened, and even more time before the gift of the Holy Spirit brought understanding and courage. Meanwhile, they had to go back to the place where they had first met Jesus, Galilee, and there rediscover him.

Perhaps we are at that stage of confusion in our lives: it will take time before we have understanding of all that's been happening and a real freedom. But if we think back to our own journeys of faith, we see that the promise of Easter is not limited to time or place but is ours always; is ours now, at this moment and so, even when we are isolated, we can truly rejoice. Jesus is risen! Alleluia!

Praise be to you, Lord Jesus Christ,
for you are risen indeed, bringing new hope and new life
and a release from guilt and a forgiveness,
a new beginning that is beyond all we can understand.

We bring to you those who are currently struggling with a
difficult, confusing time in which they feel ill, lonely, afraid.
Touch them, we pray, with your risen love.

We bring those tasked with great work and great decisions.
Touch them, we pray, with light, with the Spirit's wisdom.
We bring ourselves, seeking your light, your love within our own
lives, a love and light to share in prayer, in thought, in smile.

Thank you, Lord God our Father, for your great love.
For Jesus, who gave his life that all may have life in all its fullness.
Amen

The Walk to Emmaus

Luke 24: 13-35

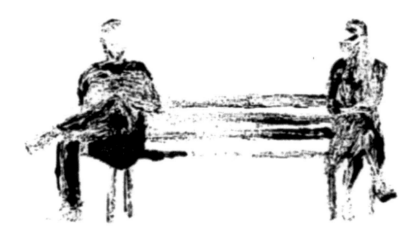

Social Distancing
© Catherine Richardson

In a way, the walk to Emmaus is a strange story to choose for reflection at this time, because although we can go for walks, we have to stay apart, and as for a stranger walking alongside us, let alone inviting them in when we get home? No way.

Yet the story does fit the times. We are walking along, mentally if not physically, wondering how all this has come about and what next. We hear theories as to how we've come to this point, but what is the truth? What do we take into the future? Our plans are in disarray. We are separated from friends and family and afraid for them, afraid for ourselves. While these and similar thoughts are bludgeoning our minds, do we recognise the risen Jesus alongside us now, this moment?

The couple on the Emmaus Road were also lost in the hows and the whys and in fears for the future, with their plans and hopes in disarray. Initially they didn't recognise Jesus, but only after they were allowed time to think; and we have the perfect opportunity now to give time for the Holy Spirit to guide us in our thinking, in choosing how we spend our time, how we react.

The recognition of Jesus came not on the road, although with hindsight they realised that they had felt something very special as he talked to them. It came after they had asked him in, and when, in sharing a meal with him, he blessed and shared the bread. This picture hurts a little, or maybe a lot. We can't meet to eat together. We can't meet to share in Holy Communion.

Maybe not physically, but our present situation gives us time to reflect; to remember that we are all connected wonderfully through Jesus, who we can daily invite into our lives. Connected together thus, we can offer each other our prayer as food and our love as drink. Our lives continue along the road that is life and in all that journey we remain closely connected. And always, always Jesus walks near to us.

For a poem that speaks very powerfully about the presence of the risen Christ in the here and now, look out for Malcolm Guite's 'Easter 2020'. I recommend it to you.

"Then their eyes were opened and they recognised him."

(Luke 24:31)

A prayer:

> Loving God, as we look back, as did Cleopas and his companion, out hearts are warmed when we remember those times our spirits have been lifted, times when a new hope bubbled up, even when the circumstances of our lives weren't good. Thank you for the words of Jesus that have inspired and re-energised us and helped us make some sense of the present

moment. May we be open always to the presence of Jesus, open to invite him within our lives.

Thank you, too, for the connection we have with Christians past and present; connection to our families and friends, even when we are not able to meet, face to face; to touch; to hug.

Lord, it is hard, not to see and to hold those who are dear to us. Give us strength to journey along this road with courage, and with hope in Jesus. We bring to you those who struggle because they are alone and ill, and those unaccustomed to being alone at all . . . those for whom we have a special concern.

Thank you, Lord, for those who have responded to the present crisis with love and commitment, all who are volunteering to help in food banks, in fetching groceries, in talking to the lonely . . . those we know who have made a difference to our own lives.

Thank you for those continuing to work, especially where that work involves some risk to themselves . . . in hospitals . . . in surgeries . . . ambulance drivers and paramedics . . . in care homes . . . in shops . . . keeping public transport running . . . policing the streets . . . so many others we bring to mind . . . be with them, we ask, be their protection, their strength.

Walk with us all, Lord Jesus. Guide all our thinking, guide all our being through the Holy Spirit, and through that same Spirit bring wisdom to those who have great decisions to make, and profound studies to carry out that the world may move forward in peace. Walk with us, and enter into our lives, our hearts, now and always.

Amen

St George's Day

S t George is Patron Saint of England, but he was born in what is now Turkey and never came to the British Isles!

A soldier who was prepared to die (by tradition in Lydda) rather than deny his Christian faith, he is venerated as a martyr all over the world. There is evidence that he was known in Great Britain from the 7th Century.

The tomb of St George in the Citadel of Aleppo, Syria
(Well, that's what we were told)

St George is, of course, famous for defeating a dragon to save a beautiful princess, his taking on the dragon dependent on the king's agreement that, should he defeat it, the people would convert to Christianity. He did, and they did. This was a story that only became current through "The Golden Legend", written about 1259-66 and printed in English by Caxton in 1483.

It's a story that carries the thought of good triumphing over evil, but the story may also connect for many of you with the story of St Michael defeating the dragon – Revelation 12: 7-12. Here the dragon is cast out of heaven down to earth to wreak its own havoc, and there's plenty of that.

This is a picture of Aleppo, taken from high on the Citadel in 2010, a smart, neat city, to compare with the pictures of shattered buildings we see today on television, a reminder that many nations are struggling against the evil of terror and war as well as the COVID-19 virus. 'Dragons' do not always come singly!

But in spite of all this, perhaps the story of George and his dragon has something of encouragement to say to us today, as we face our own 'dragons'. These may be fierce worries about our families and friends, or worries about money, or worries about health, or worries about the state of the world. Or perhaps the COVID-19 virus itself appears as a kind of dragon. Pause and be still. Have courage.

Read Ephesians 6: 10-20 – the Armour of God

We can take on this armour ourselves and, as someone once said, it's all armour to protect our front – we face whatever there is before us with courage, for Christ is risen. Light and love have defeated the power of darkness, and hope lives, always.

A prayer:

When many of us were children, we sang the hymn, When a knight won his spurs. Oh, for the day we can truly sing, "For the knights are no more, and the dragons are dead," for we are only too aware that the dragons of anger, of war, of illness still roam our world.

We remember before you, Loving God, those places where war and terror are still part of life, thinking particularly of Syria, of Israel and Palestine, of so many places where there is conflict of any kind. We bring families pushed close together because of Lockdown, those in crowded refugee camps.

Lord, bring the peace that Jesus offers, we pray, the peace that the world cannot give. Thank you that you offer us the strength and courage to face whatever comes, and thank you, too, that you have promised that you will never give us more than we can cope with, though we confess that sometimes, Lord, it seems to us too much.

We bring those who are struggling with illness at this time, Lord, bring your healing peace to all, we pray. With them, we bring those working within hospitals, hospices, GP surgeries, district nurses, carers, and so many more . . . and for those who work in shops, who carry out deliveries, and so many more . . .
May they know the strength and peace of the presence of Christ to uphold and enfold them.

Lord, we thank you for those who are simply a smiling, loving presence as they go about the world, defeating sadness and gloom by the lightness they bring. Help us know that small victories over darkness are each significant to you, and to the bringing of your kingdom of peace and justice to our world.

Help us live in the power of your Spirit with new courage, new hope, new love. We ask it in the name of Jesus, your Son, our Saviour.

Amen

Back to Normal?

© Helen E Gordon

John 21: 1-17

As we wait to see what next with Lockdown, most folk long for things to go back to normal but many tell us that life afterwards will be different, and there is concern as to what that 'different' might be. In a way, the disciples were in the same position – life had followed a particular pattern of being alongside Jesus on his itinerant ministry, but then came the shock of his arrest and crucifixion, and although they now knew that he was alive and with them in a special way, there would have been fear of arrest still and a huge void of unknowing if they thought about the future. It's that void of unknowing that was the problem and is for us, too.

So Peter decided to go back to normal life, to the fishing he'd known so well for years, and probably been quite good at. It was a living, certainly!

"I am going out fishing," said Peter, and the other fishermen said they'd go too. Made sense. Back to what we understand. So how, I wonder, did they feel when they'd been out all night and caught precisely zilch? That had certainly happened to them in the past, but in the state of confusion they were in, it must have been tempting to say, "And we're no good at this anymore!"

But, guided by Jesus, they tried again and made this huge catch, only recognising him as they were struggling to get it all to the shore.

At this point, it's easy to get diverted by questions such as what does the number of fish mean and how Jesus had already got fish cooking ready for them. Let's leave those questions aside, as they're not helpful at the moment. What matters here and now for us is the fact that Jesus showed that he could turn around any situation for them, and the way in which Peter found an assurance that he had a new, very significant part to play in the future. Not an easy role, but one that Jesus needed him and trusted him to take up.

So, back to normal? In a world where we find that 'normality' has shifted, we get on with life as it is in the here and now and wait for the guidance we need, this moment and in the future.

Some questions to bring quietly and prayerfully before God:

- Back to normal? What is 'normal'?
- What is 'normal' for me, for my neighbour and for the Church
- Where and what are my fears and my longings?

A prayer:

> Living, loving God, thank you for the normality of so much in our lives – our homes, our relationships with those dear to us, relationships that remain strong, even when we are physically

separated. Nature, in our gardens and outside our windows, just getting on with living. Thank you, Lord, for the signs of continuing life and thank you for the things that bind us together, for families finding time for each other, to talk together, to share questions and seek answers. To just be.

Yet although there is so much that is normal, our lives feel very abnormal. We bring those who are afraid for the future, afraid that their livelihood has crashed about their ears, afraid that their dreams are shattered and unachievable, afraid that already shaky relationships will shatter completely.

We bring those for whom normality has long ago fled: those in nations beset by war and terror, by flood, by famine . . . refugees, thinking especially at this time of the several Refugee Services, praying a response to the requests for financial aid.

We bring also the local Food Banks and food distribution centres, those working to distribute supplies and those needing their services.

Loving Lord, there is so much that confuses us today. May your Spirit guide our thinking and, most especially, the thinking of all those who have hard decisions to make that will affect us all. And for ourselves and all people, we pray: When we are frustrated with the present moment, Living God, give us your calm. When we are afraid for the future, Loving God, give us your peace. May Jesus be with us to guide, and with those we love, today and always.

We offer this prayer in his name.
Amen

**Jesus is risen! Light and love triumph
over darkness; hope lives again.**

Feeling Scared

John 20: 19-21

After weeks in Lockdown, in some cases being told not to go out at all, even for walks, and as Government discusses what next, opinion polls tell us that people are now feeling frightened at the thought of leaving the house. This is actually quite logical, because in a relatively short time we have had to learn to fear what is outside: the unseen virus. Although there are exceptions, it's relatively easy to frighten people with an unknown 'out there', even scary skies! After all, it's the staple of the horror film. And knowing how it is to become ill at the same time as looking at the data, we know that the Lockdown is the sensible way to control the rate of infection. So being inside now feels very safe.

At this point, it's worth looking at the disciples, locked away in what many believe was the Upper Room on the Sunday evening. They were frightened to the extent that they'd locked themselves in, frightened of what could happen to them outside. What might that be? Worst-case scenario, arrest and trial and some kind of punishment. Best case scenario, perhaps ostracism. And I'm sure that, being normal human beings, they felt a whole range of nameless fears.

Bear in mind that this was the evening of the day they'd heard that Jesus was alive, so that you'd expect them to be full of hope and joy; but fear is a very strong emotion, and group fear stronger still, while night is the time when it seems to have its strongest hold over us.

Then Jesus came to them, in the room with its locked door, and said, "Peace."

I think that "Peace," isn't just a greeting or a statement that it's all going to be alright. It carries the sense of an inner calm that keeps us from letting our imaginations run riot; the calm that lets us look at what might come next without all the "but-but-buts" that stop us from thinking clearly. John tells us that Jesus next breathed on them, saying "receive the Holy Spirit." There was going to be a future in which they were going to have to face a lot and do a lot of difficult stuff and Jesus gave them the calm and peace they were going to need. I suspect that we're going to need peace, calm and the wisdom of the Spirit too in the days, weeks and months ahead.

But it's interesting as we think that Jesus had been with the disciples to guide them and help them out in the world, and now he was with them in the locked room.

Jesus is with us, wherever we might be, is with us when we lock ourselves away in our inner selves. His peace, that inner calm he offers to us, and brings that gift of the Spirit, is ours too.

Poet Hilaire Belloc's "Cautionary Tales" includes Jim – who ran away from his Nurse and was eaten by a Lion, (it's more fun than it sounds), a poem that ends with the advice from the boy's father, who,

'Bade all the children round attend
To James' miserable end,
And always keep a-hold of Nurse
For fear of finding something worse.'

To reflect – how much do we unconsciously follow this advice as adults, though we might phrase it differently, and what does it mean to take Jesus' gift of peace into the situations where we fear 'something worse'? In the worry and uncertainty of the present moment, pause to hear Jesus offering his peace to you. His inner calm. Reflect on those you know who are desperately in need of that peace within, and seek that blessing for them.

A prayer:

In the safety of our homes, we come to you, Lord God our Father, for you love and understand us beyond all our imagining and deserving. We come thankful for Jesus, for the love that took him through death to win a new, eternal life for us. Thankful, too, for the gift of the Holy Spirit who brings understanding and comfort, peace to our disordered emotions and lives. Within the safety of our homes, we seek your blessing upon the homes of our neighbours, our families and our friends, that the peace Jesus brings may rest upon them, today and always. We seek, too, that peace for those homes where there is conflict and violence, mental and physical, those places where home is not a safe haven, but a place of fear, fear inside and fear of the world beyond.

Thank you for those who have broken down the barriers of isolation through telephone conversations, through use of the internet, through letters, through exchanging a smile or a word, and thank you for the knowledge that we do not have to be physically together in order to know the deep connection we have one with another, in Jesus. The church continues, lives, will live anew. We praise and thank you, Lord, for that truth.

Aware that it is the disadvantaged who have fallen ill in greater numbers, we pray for justice for all people in the time to come.

Loving Lord God, we know that sometimes we must emerge from our own safety to speak out for others. Give us wisdom and courage, we pray.

Lord God, to all who are afraid, bring your peace and calm. To all who have big decisions to make that affect us all, bring your calm and wisdom. To us all, bring peace, calm and the wisdom to live well.

Amen

Christian Aid Week

St Mark 7: 24-37

It's hard when we're struggling here in this country to remember the suffering of others around the world.

But the truth is that we can't forget that we are all people together. Often we do think how fortunate we are in Lockdown if we have gardens, decent sized houses, places to walk, and we think sadly about folk restricted to home with none of these. Yet perhaps less often we remember that COVID-19 is also hitting nations already beset by all kinds of natural disaster, and by disaster caused by humans. There are so many lands in which health care is already at breaking-point, where the work of Christian Aid and other charities matters so much.

The problem is that we all have a natural tendency to turn in upon ourselves and 'our' people: many have observed and spoken about trends towards a greater selfishness, "tribalism", in the world which leads to a tendency to see "the other" as an enemy. It's an impulse that affects us all, but how we respond can make all the difference to us and to others.

For one thing, don't we need to share the knowledge and resources we have to conquer the Corona Virus Lockdown?

The passage I've suggested we read can be interpreted as showing that even Jesus was hesitant to take his work beyond his own Jewish people: that response to the Gentile Syro-Phoenician woman is sharp. However, her response was equally sharp and quick-witted, and Jesus responded, healing her daughter. I've suggested reading further because the next healing that is noted is of a deaf man who has full hearing restored, and the impediment to his speech removed. That's an interesting pairing. We have a child who is 'possessed' – maybe by voices, can't be still, can't think clearly - and she is calmed, then we have a man who lives in a silent world, unable to hear at all and whose speech stumbles. He has real hearing and speech restored, to use. He hears the voices of others, and joins his voice to theirs.

We are pretty anxious today and maybe that anxiety stops us hearing the truth in all the competing voices in society and in the media and makes us stumble in our attempts to speak out.

So we pray. We pray for the peace that Christ can bring to us and for God's guiding Spirit as we listen and as we speak, for we each need our own healing.

When we have a measure of peace and our hearing opened up – to hear the cry of the powerless, the cry of suffering – does it not also loosen up our tongues to speak out? Or, in the modern world, our fingers to type out an email? Or a Tweet? Or to make a donation to Christian Aid, or to the Refugee Service or to the local Foodbank?

Time now to reflect on John Donne's famous poem. I make no apology for writing this out in full.

Read it slowly, with its reminder that the loss of the least significant, in worldly terms, makes a difference to us all. We can turn that around: the small, good act also makes a difference to us all!

> The bell, tolling softly for another, says to me:
> Thou must die.
> As therefore the bell that rings to a sermon
> calls not upon the preacher only
> but upon the congregation to come,
> so this bell calls us all.
> No man is an island, entire of itself;
> every man is a piece of the continent, a part of the main.
> If a clod be washed away by the sea
> Europe is the less
> as well as if a promontory were.
> Any man's death diminishes me
> because I am involved in mankind,
> And therefore, never send to know for whom the bell tolls:
> It tolls for thee.

Let's think of those who live in lands where famine, war, disease, drought and terrible poverty have destroyed so much. And let's think thankfully of those who try to make a difference, helping people rebuild their lives, giving them the tools to start again.

So we pray.

Living Lord God, we bring to you those who we have remembered, whose value in your eyes is as great as the richest and most powerful. We pray your blessing upon them, your love to surround them, your healing to fill them. In a world in which some have far more than they need and very many have nothing, we mourn the injustice that fills our world and pray strength for those people and organisations that work tirelessly to bring about change, in our own nation as well as abroad, and pray that your Spirit may touch the ears of the powerful that they might hear the small voice of the powerless and respond in the common good.

God of the impossible, we pray for justice, peace and reconciliation. And when the challenges seem too many, remind us of your resurrection power, and the miracles of your love that happen, whenever justice is dismantled and rebuilt with peace. Help us live within that peace – peace of heart, peace in relationships, peace in all creation, that we may hear the call of the bird, the buzz of the insect, the whirl of the wind, with joy, and speak out and sing with equal joy and love, We ask it in the name of Jesus your Son, who died and rose again that all may have life in all its fullness.

Amen

Ascension Day

Acts 1: 1-11

If we'd been living in Medieval times, we would all be going to church on Ascension Day to a service rather different to any we might experience today. Of course, they might well have gone worrying about catching some illness, so maybe there are some similarities . . . but what they might have seen is not what we may expect. We probably know that churches had Biblical stories painted on the walls, to tell these stories to a largely illiterate congregation, but as well as this, the stories were acted out at the major festivals. Thus, on Ascension Day, you may well have seen the statue of Jesus which normally stood in the church, wrapped round with ropes that extended to the ceiling so that at a given point in the service it could be hoisted through the trapdoor in the ceiling – literally ascending, as lilies were thrown down from above to represent the clouds. It must have been fun.

But, of course, unrealistic. Vast telescopes that reach far, far into space have shown that this galaxy in which our little planet travels is enormous, and that there are other galaxies beyond and beyond . . . it gives you a headache thinking about it. And then, of course, there is space travel; we have sent men to the moon; we send probes to Mars and beyond, so that people now say, "Heaven isn't up there!"

But it's not bad imagery, is it, because we use up and down language daily. Lift up your hearts. Light-hearted. Cheer up! Down in the dumps. Depression. I'm sure you can think of more examples.

And looking out and up does help us. The heavens, the sky, are glorious. The changing colours of the sky, hour by hour; sunrise; sunset; the black storm clouds – all these catch our breath, and as for a night sky peppered with stars: wow! I don't mind admitting that among my photographs are a fair number that are just of the sky. No earth, just sky.

And if the sky is so glorious, what about the creator of the heavens? Perhaps in our wordy non-conformist way we find it hard to focus on the glory of God; just to pause and be aware of his might; his power; his incredible beauty, and that is something we need to focus on today.

It's very easy, today, to be worried about infection and death rates, about the Lockdown and how we ease out of it, about the church and society in the 'new normal', a phrase being bandied about a great deal. Let's be honest: the disciples could have nicely used the same phrase, for they were certainly in a state of new normality – and at this stage, they had no more idea of what that 'new normal' might be than we have.

In our reading, the disciples believed heaven was up there; they believed Jesus had ascended into heaven – why not keep looking up; longing? It must have been very tempting to stay, looking up at what had been and hoping, hoping . . . but they were shooed away from sky-gazing by the two men in white, just as, in Luke's account of the resurrection, the women were turned away from the tomb (Luke 24:4-9). Luke means us to connect the two events. Don't hang around here worrying – go back, and wait.

Wait, prayerfully and watchfully, for the next stage.

The new way for the disciples might not imitate the past, but would draw upon it, and I think we need to keep this in mind when we're getting very anxious about the future. This week, let's look up and beyond in our prayers, for the glory and love of God are greater than all our experience, and the presence of Christ eternal.

It will probably help us to physically look towards the furthest horizon we can – or look at pictures that include a lot of sky or sea - to symbolically remind us that what is immediately around us is not all there is; that our worries are not all that we are.

Living Lord God, we lift our eyes to you, for you are glorious. Ascended Jesus, our Saviour, we lift our eyes to you, for you are glorious. Vibrant Spirit, we lift our eyes to you, for you are

glorious. Lift up, we pray, those whose gaze is heavy, weighed
down by care –
* those we know who are ill or in mourning,
* those who are weary, caring for the sick and suffering,
* those who are finding their faith crumbling,
* those who don't know where the next meal will come from,
* those who are fearful, and whose fear
manifests itself in violence,
* those who are fearful, and whose fear turns
them in on themselves,
* those who are weighed down by decisions.

And with thanksgiving we bring those who bring joy, who make
us laugh and give us new hope.
Our prayers we offer in Jesus' name.

Amen

Loving God, lift our minds above our worries to the glory and
wonder beyond us. Guide us, keep us, and all those who are in
our thoughts, near and far away, powerful or powerless.

We ask it in Jesus' name.
Amen

Ascension Window

Jesmond United
Reformed Church

Pentecost

Acts 2: 1-21

Joyful, prayerful, but getting on with a bit of admin as they waited to see what next (Acts 1: 12-26), on the day of Pentecost the disciples discovered that 'next' was mind-blowing in the nicest sense of the word. The coming upon them of the Holy Spirit as a mighty wind and as fire began to open their minds to understand Jesus in a deeper, fuller way and began to give them courage to move forward into the new place God needed them to be. In Peter's case, that meant speaking out with a new courage. For all of them, it meant withstanding the sniggers of the crowd.

Pentecost is, of course, one of the great festivals of the Church, and it feels very peculiar, not to say wrong, to imagine not being in church to celebrate. But let's go back a step.

The Holy Spirit had been active since the beginning of time (Genesis 1:2), but in the Old Testament the Spirit was given to individuals for specific tasks, Moses being an example.

When Moses became very weary with leading an often-recalcitrant people through the wilderness (and who wouldn't?) God said he would take some of the Spirit granted to Moses and give it to seventy of the Elders. Accordingly, the Elders prepared themselves and gathered with Moses at the Tent of Meeting outside the camp and received the gift of the Spirit and prophesied. So far so good. But two Elders, Eldad and Medad, had dodged the column for whatever reason and stayed in the camp – and the Spirit fell upon them, too, and they prophesied, much to the horror of a young man who ran out to tell Moses. Fine for the Elders to be embarrassing outside the camp, but at home? Please, no! Moses responded, "Would that all God's people were prophets and that the Lord would put his spirit on them!" (Read it all in Numbers 11: 16-30)

God wanted and needed those Elders to receive the Spirit, and found them, wherever they were, together or alone.

You may remember a text that was popular in Victorian times as an embroidery to be hung over the bed-head, "Thou, God seest me." A boy, afraid at the thought of God always seeing him confided his fear to his Grandmother.

"Well, what it is," she said, "is that he loves you so much, he can't take his eyes off you!"

God loves us so much he can't take his eyes off us and longs for us to receive the Holy Spirit, wherever we might be, in company or alone, in church, at home, or out for a walk. The Spirit that will lead us into fuller understanding and discernment, a gift really needed today! But note I say 'fuller', not full understanding – our understanding of the current situation, of people, of ourselves, even, is always incomplete.

The Spirit also brings, wonderfully, peace and real joy. God longs for us to have all this. Today, let's remember that Moses' wish that the Spirit would fall upon all people began to come true at the Day of Pentecost. Let's open ourselves to receive and be joyful, wherever we are.

You might like to try reading Numbers 11: 24-30 slowly, trying to imagine yourself into the story.

Who are you in the story? An Elder who went out, as instructed, to stand around the Tent of Meeting, the holy place? Imagine the quietness of the desert after the noise of the crowded camp, the wind blowing gently – and then this transformative change; this shock that makes you cry out in praise of God, to see your place in sharing the task laid upon Moses . . . or perhaps you are Eldad or Medad – why are you staying away? Did you just forget? Did you not want the responsibility? And then that shock – God knows and sees you, and wants you to have an equal gift . . .

You may also like to read Acts 2: 1-21 in the same way, but if you imagine yourself in the crowd, what do you think of all these others around you, these people from places with strange-sounding names? Resentful or glad that they're sharing in this experience of seeing people transformed, of seeing God moving so powerfully? What are your own deep feelings as you think of your own life transformed?

Pause, and spend some time in quiet, trying not to think or worry. (Not easy!)

And so we pray:

Holy Spirit of God, joyfully we remember your coming upon the disciples at Pentecost and recall thankfully the promise that you come to all people, as we open our hearts and minds.

Holy Spirit of God, coming as fire, burn up we pray, our guilt at all we sometimes do and are, and our guilt at our part in the sin of the world, all that is contrary to the will of the Father . . . which we bring to mind, and so before you. Help us hear Jesus' gentle words, "Your sins are forgiven."

Holy Spirit of God, coming as wind, blow us along the pathways we need to walk, the ways we need to go that the Kingdom of Peace and Justice may come. As we recall the story of the Elders outside and within the camp, we think of the many people who are today crowded within refugee camps, fearful and weary, and all people, at home and abroad within houses as little secure as tents in the wilderness, people not knowing what the future will bring. We pray for them . . .

Holy Spirit of God, blow through the corridors of power, we pray, that the powerful may hear the sighs of these, the powerless, and fan to flame a passion for true justice and action.

Holy Spirit of God, coming as the dove, may your soft wings touch with healing power those who are ill at this time, whether in body, mind or situation. We think of those who are terrified at the thought of contracting Coronavirus . . . those in hospital, very ill, or recovering . . . those in care homes . . . those distraught at not being able to physically visit those dear to them who are ill . . . those who mourn . . .

Holy Spirit of God you bring wisdom, you bring peace: bring true wisdom and peace, we pray, to all the world in these troubled times.

We ask it in Jesus' name.
Amen

Trinity Sunday

The Garden of the Forty Martyrs, Sinai

Be watchful!

Matthew 26: 41

How is being watchful different to being alert, as we're being called to do by the Government? In one way it's not so different, but I think being watchful is a wider term that suggests a taking time, as the person in the picture is doing, to look, to really see and to reflect on what we see.

There are many calls to be watchful in the Bible, and some beautiful passages that speak of watching eagerly – Psalm 130 is one of my particular favourites, with the repeated phrase:

"my soul waits for the Lord more than those who watch for the morning." (Psalm 130:5-6)

But the passage I can't get out of my head at the moment is the parable of the Ten Bridesmaids. (Matthew 25:1-13) They were supposed to be awake (alert, even!) and ready to welcome the bridegroom home, and five fulfilled the task and five didn't, sleepy and unprepared.

It seems to me that circumstances have inevitably led us to focus almost entirely in one direction, COVID-19, while other things have been happening that require our prayer and perhaps that we be ready for what comes. The relationship of Beijing and Hong Kong; annexation of sections of the Occupied Territories; the current racial tension in the USA; floundering talks with the EU and the real possibility of a hard Brexit – and I'm sure you can think of others. Then add the tensions most people are feeling at the relaxation of Lockdown. In many ways we're like the person in the picture, peering over the wall at the harsh terrain beyond. Maybe we don't want to look, which is entirely understandable, but I believe we need to keep watching, uncomfortable though it may be.

It doesn't always have to be uncomfortable, though; there are positives out there too. Air pollution is down because we haven't used cars and planes so much. People have been walking regularly, families out together talking and noticing the world around them. That's all great, and we long for it to spill over into the post-COVID-19 world.

If we're to look out for God in our world, God in creation, in human interaction and love, in the push for justice for all peoples, God in threefold nature of Father, Son and Spirit (I hadn't forgotten it's Trinity Sunday this Sunday), we have to face both good and bad so that our prayer and actions can be informed and deeply connected. Watch and pray, prepared, always.

God in Trinity is a reminder of the Unity inherent in the Godhead, a unity we long to see in humankind.

A prayer that went onto the posters I made this week alongside these thoughts and prayer:

Let's give thanks – for creation, for people we love, for people trying to make the world a better place. And we offer our worries for creation, for all people, for the world. May God guide us into peace today and always. Amen

So let's pray:

Living God, one in the eternal unity of Father, Son and Spirit, we praise and bless you. Your love for all creation reaches to the farthest heights and plumbs the deepest depths, and we pause in awe at the power and beauty of that love. Beside it, our love is partial, erratic: we want to be and do the best possible, but fail, again and again. Yet again and again you lift us up and enable us, through the power of the Spirit, to begin once more, forgiven, freed, offered life in all its fullness through the death and resurrection of Jesus. In that confidence, we bring to you our watching and waiting.

* we bring the new places we have found to walk, or the usual pathways that you can make unusual by giving us new appreciation, new insight . . .
* we bring the families that have been able to find a new unity through talking and learning together, that the closeness they have enjoyed may live on . . . and we bring those families for whom being together has enlarged existing fractures . . . we pray, Lord, your healing presence, your peace.
* we bring nations facing crisis upon crisis and hesitant as they face an uncertain future . . . living Lord, we pray the wisdom of the Spirit and the humility to listen, to admit fault, to learn.
* we bring those who are particularly upon our hearts and minds, whether close to us or seen only on the

television screen or heard of through radio . . . in a troubled world, we pray peace.
* and with joy we bring those able to reconnect with family, those enjoying the freedom of the outside world, the wonder of who we are and what we can be.

And finally, the last verse of the hymn,[+]
'Come Holy Ghost our souls inspire':
Teach us to know the Father, Son
and thee, of both to be but One,
that through the ages all along
this may be our endless song,
'Praise to thine eternal merit,
Father, Son, and Holy Spirit'.

Amen

[+]9th Century, translated John Cosin (1594-1672)

Shepherds

Matthew 9: 35 – 10: 8

I'm drawing on the Gospel reading for this Sunday, particularly Verse 36 of chapter 9 which leapt out at me:

> *"When he saw the crowds, he had compassion for them, because they were harassed and helpless, like sheep without a shepherd"*

At the moment many people feel adrift, the regulations are changing so quickly and sometimes confusedly. We are told that the 'R' number must remain under 1. Very sensible, but in Cumbria, where my sister lives and where people are now allowed to visit on days out, the R number has risen to 1.1 as I write this. Harassed and helpless seems to sum it up rather well.

But the impact of this verse was heightened because John Bunyan's *Pilgrim's Progress* has been on my mind, a book written in a stressful situation that imagines the difficulties faced by the Christian (well, anyone, really) on their path through life. The section that especially came to mind was that in which Christian and his companion Hopeful are helped by the Shepherds who are called Knowledge, Experience, Watchful and Sincere, names that in themselves deserve a pause to reflect, for they are surely essential qualities for this time. Which do we have? Which is lacking?

The Shepherds take the two men into the mountains where they are able to get some perspective on the way ahead, but this is no pleasant sight-seeing excursion, for they are shown not only the pathway ahead but also the difficulties and disastrous consequences if they make wrong choices along the way. They are shown that there will be no safe short-cuts. And they have no Sat-nav!

After being shown the hazards they must face, Christian and Hopeful are trusted with a glimpse of their destination when the Shepherds decide to let them look through a 'perspective glass' (a telescope) to see the Celestial Gate to which they are travelling. However, they have been so terrified by seeing the awful things that would await them if they went astray that their hands tremble so that they "could not look steadily through the glass; yet they thought they saw something like the Gate, and also some of the glory of the place."

Now, sometimes we are given brief glimpses of the glory and beauty of what is to come in the life beyond this, but I think this picture also applies to the difficulty of looking ahead to the place we long to reach here and now. We have predictions and our own vision of what the 'new normal' will be, but no clarity.

What I find heartening is the verse from Matthew's Gospel quoted above. "The sight of the crowd moved Jesus to pity." Jesus was travelling about, preaching, teaching and healing the sick, people very lost and anxious and hassled, just like us. He was busy – but his heart went out to them. It's a hugely loving picture for us to hold close to our own hearts.

I'm sure you've had the experience where you've seen someone struggling, perhaps at work, perhaps with family and there comes the point where they burst into tears or throw a wobbly, and you can get in there and comfort and really help. It's then that they see there is something beyond their struggling, and that there is help along the way. I guess the more hassled we are, the more Jesus' heart goes out to us to pour his love into our lives. Keep your eyes ahead and upon him, and allow the Holy Spirit to guide you through a pathway that does not promise to be easy.

Pray, and keep your vision clear.

Having 'shepherded' people across the Pilgrims' Way over the sands to Holy Island, I know how much thought needs to go into the planning and how joyful the sight of the horizon ahead. We may not be able to see the way ahead yet, but it will come.

Holy Island Causeway
at high tide ... and low tide

A prayer:

Loving, living God and Father, in hope, we look beyond ourselves to creation, earth and sky, and praise and bless you for the distant horizon which lifts our spirits when we are low, and for that far, far horizon that leads beyond this life, a horizon crossed by Jesus, opening the way to full eternal life.

We praise and bless you for your love shown in Jesus, a love that gives to the utmost, a heart that breaks in pity for the struggles of we, the harassed and helpless who stumble and fall, longing to be better people, longing to walk by right pathways. We pray for those who are struggling to find ways through the current crises, here and throughout the world, crises not only caused by coronavirus but by the injustices and lack of peace suffered by so many, whether in society or in the family.

In hope, we look beyond ourselves to the care and love shown by others, the pieces of your love that rest within all our hearts. We bring those we know who have shown an exceptional love . . . and those who struggle along, not thinking they are anything special, but who make a massive difference to the lives of many . . . and we bring those who mourn; who are ill; who are afraid . . . asking your healing peace.

In hope, we look beyond ourselves to the pathway we walk today, through crises near and far away and to those who walk this pathway with us. We pray the guiding presence of the Holy Spirit for all who have great decisions to make today . . . that their hearts may be moved to pity, and minds sharpened to see the way ahead . . . and we give you thanks, Lord our God, that you love and guide us all, always.

Amen

Truth

Matthew 12: 22-30

Y̶ou may be feeling a little like this just now. Or if you aren't, many people are. Barraged by information, instructions changing day by day, news worrying us, people are saying, "I just don't know what to believe – or who to believe." Where is the truth?

I passed two ladies even more elderly than myself having a conversation across their garden, and it was fairly clear they'd been talking about Dominic Cummings' journey to Durham. "Well," said one, "I think all we can do is keep doing the right thing ourselves," which brings in another question – where does my own common sense enter into it all?

Much of our difficulty lies in the fact that we know that we do lie to one another (oh, yes we do!), and often for the kindest of reasons - Santa Claus, the Tooth Fairy et al are obvious candidates, but what about the Little White Lies we tell to spare feelings? But sometimes the lies are manipulative and decidedly suspect and I think we're becoming more aware of how easily we can be manipulated by those with even a little power. Gaslighting is the in-phrase for this.

This is not a new phenomenon. When Jesus was healing people and the crowds were gathering to hear his teaching, those opposed to him basically began a smear campaign, "it is only by Beelzebul, the ruler of the demons, that this fellow casts out devils". (Matthew 12:24) You can understand the unease felt when the people heard those they trusted, the Pharisees, suggesting that what they thought was of God actually had a basis in evil. Jesus was absolutely clear where his power came from, and answered his detractors well, but it must have shaken the security of ordinary folk.

Later, Pontius Pilate would ask, "What is truth?" (John 18:28) Truth, we know, was literally standing in front of him, weary and battered, but unrecognisable to a man who dealt in power and in hanging onto his own authority. Truth does not always show itself through strength and power, though truth is there for all to find.

But how do we discern truth here and now? The key word there is 'discern', one of the wonderful gifts of the Holy Spirit. We who follow Jesus who we believe is the Way, the Truth and the Life, have, I strongly believe, an obligation to seek truth first in our own words and lives, and then in the words of the powerful and, if we can, to call out untruths as and where we are able. Only by a reliance on this gift of discernment, praying for the insight it gives, can we be equipped to do so. The world needs us to do this.

And our own common sense? I think good old common sense is linked to the gifts of the Spirit. It's an inner warning system to which we should all attend.

Pause, and remember those people you've known who had little in worldly terms, but had great wisdom. People who spoke truth to you.

Praise God that people still stand with Jesus, and speak truth, always.

We pray that we might do likewise.

Let's pray, using first some words of Launcelot Andrewes (1555-1626)

I exist. I am alive. I have a mind. Lord, my Lord, I praise you.

For my upbringing and education, for my instruction in the Christian Way, for the qualities and abilities you have given me, Lord, my Lord, I praise you.

For the success I have had, for all the good I have received from others for my present situation and future hopes, Lord, my Lord, I praise you.

For my parents, well-wishers and friends, for those who have helped me by their books, words, prayers, example, tellings off, Lord, my Lord, I praise you.

How can I repay you for all your gifts to me? What thanks can I give for all your patience and love?

Loving Lord God and Father, we offer our prayer, our yearning that the world may one day be filled with your peace, your truth, your love.

Amen

Lord Jesus, Way, Truth and Life, we bring those trying to make sense of the conflicting views given them day by day, and we bring those who have great power and responsibility in the shaping of public opinion . . . We bring those who try to speak a word of truth in the corridors of power and within the media . . .and those who speak words of truth and comfort to family and neighbours . .

Holy Spirit, guide and comfort all, we pray.
Loving God, Father, Son and Spirit, we lift our gaze to the wider world, to people oppressed in unjust regimes . . . to areas where there is great conflict . . . places where the activity of the unjust goes unnoticed by the world while each nation looks to their own crises . . .
God in unity, draw us together that we may see our own connection with all humankind.

Holy Spirit, bring wisdom, bring compassion, bring listening ears and hearts, we pray. Eternal God, Father Son and Spirit, one in perfect unity, the pain of the world is your pain too, for you love us with a perfect love. Help us hold to this great truth and to act upon it, today and always.

Amen

A Common Humanity

Deuteronomy 16: 9-15
Matthew 10: 40-42

> *'We appear to be living in a world characterised increasingly by fury,*
> *in which we yell ever more loudly at one another*
> *while the distance between us only grows.'*
>
> John Sutherland
> *Crossing the Line, Lessons from a Life on Duty*
> 2020 Weidenfeld and Nicholson

These words by former Chief Superintendent of the Metropolitan Police, John Sutherland, have a truth for our time. Indeed, it does seem to be he or she who shouts loudest who makes it to the top, and he or she who encourages separation – them and us, with us always right – who finds a ready audience. And beneath it all lurks anger.

If you think I'm wrong, think back to the rise in abusive behaviour towards those assumed to be immigrants after the Brexit vote. Or the rhetoric of Donald Trump and others. Or the unrest seen in the streets today. Or the fact that the economically and socially disadvantaged areas and the Black, Asian and Minority Ethnic groups are hit far more severely by the COVID-19 virus. We don't like to think it, but our society is divided.

If we turn to the Bible, we find a far different aim. In the Old Testament we often see the people instructed to care for the stranger, the orphan, the widow and, in the passage above, the instruction to celebrate harvest includes everyone.

Then we have St Paul, who mixed easily with Jews and Gentiles, men and women (Yes, check it out!); the escaped slave Onesimus was his friend, as was Onesimus' master, Philemon. (Letter to Philemon). Yes, he urged slaves, wives and children to be obedient, but he didn't follow the crowd in that he also urged masters, husbands and fathers to treat everyone with true compassion (Ephesians 5:21-6:9). To treat everyone as fellow human beings. Then there is this lovely passage:

> *"There is no longer Jew or Greek, there is no longer slave or free, there is no longer male and female; for all of you are one in Christ Jesus."*
>
> (Galatians 3:28)

In 1766 Ignatius Sancho, an African freedman born on a slave-ship but now enjoying fame among the literati of London society, came across a sermon critical of slavery given by Laurence Sterne, clergyman author of *Tristram Shandy*, and wrote to him encouraging him to speak out further. This Sterne did in his next novel, *A Sentimental Journey through France and Italy*, only two volumes of which were completed before his death. In it the narrator, Parson Yorick, in Paris visiting the Bastille, hears a cry, "I can't get out," and traces it to a starling in a cage, the bird repeating the cry over and over. He struggles to untangle the "twisted and double twisted" wires that seal the cage door but, "there was no getting it open without pulling the cage to pieces." "No," said the starling, "I can't get out." The image caught the attention of many. It catches my attention.

Contemporary writers speak of their concern at a trend to terrible demonisation of one group by another, and of the profound divisions in our world today. If we look at this alongside the call to see ourselves as one with all humanity we may feel that helplessness, knowing that the whole structure must change, but we're not able to unpick it. Yet.

We may feel we are as ineffective as Yorick struggling to open the cage, but we can keep sheltering, caring for each other, keep trying, praying, working away bit by bit. Like Paul, we make relationships in our own lives and communities that build up rather than tear down, for Jesus himself tells us that the small action matters. We learn to protect others, to rescue, to just be there for one another, whether near at hand or far away. And we value the contribution of the least among us.

© Helen E Gordon

A prayer:

Living Lord God and Father, the earth and all within it are yours. We rest within your great love that holds all in being, a love that sent Jesus to share our life, making the small changes within a limited place and time that blossomed into a new way of living and being, and that brought to us, through his death and resurrection, the hope of new, vibrant, eternal life.

We praise and bless you for those who reflect upon the world and respond through word and image to help us see ourselves and society through new eyes.

Through the power of your Holy Spirit we ask, with some trepidation, that we may see ourselves and society through *your* eyes. We bring the conflicts within our own society and throughout the world . . . Remembering our common humanity, we mourn the divisions and inequalities that fuel a helplessness that in turn fuels anger . . . the greed and lust for power that motivates so much hurt . . . the fear that causes nations to see enemies beyond their borders . . .

"My peace I give to you," said Jesus. We earnestly pray that same peace to fill our world. We bring the Church, seeking to show the way of inclusive peace, especially at this time when we are physically unable to meet together in worship . . . when our buildings can look bleak, closed and shabby . . .

May the Spirit guide all in positions of leadership in our debate and decisions as we seek to find new, right ways of resuming our life together, safely.

We bring our own neighbourhoods, with all their joys and tensions, remembering those who are going through hard times because of ill health or economic fears . . . and with them, in thanksgiving, we bring our families and the friends who are as family to us . . . asking blessing and, where it is needed, healing peace . . .

And with joy and thanksgiving we remember that we each have a place and a task that helps one another, be it ever so small.

Guide and bless us as we break down barriers between us and find new hope, in Jesus' name.

Amen

Easing out of Lockdown

Numbers 13: 17-33
Matthew 11: 25-30

© Helen E Gordon

When I lived in Amble, I was sufficiently foolish to take on someone else's stray cat as well as the one I had already. He was a tough, street-wise city cat for whom the appearance of a dog in the back lane was no more than an interesting challenge. Unremarkably, ere long few dogs ventured into our back lane. But when I married and moved to

Warkworth, he could be seen, less tough, peering nervously through the fence at the open space of the adjacent field. New normal, no less! Of course, being resourceful, he quickly accommodated himself to it.

After months of accommodating ourselves to rules protecting us against a deadly virus, we seem to be moving swiftly on to something different. The sudden turn-arounds and conflicting views from those who are supposed to know does nothing for our confidence, or lack of. In general, many of us have decided to rely on our own common sense and proceed with caution.

The Biblical connection that has struck me is that section of the Exodus story where Moses sent spies into the Promised Land to check it out, and they came back with conflicting views. A wonderful land flowing with milk and honey, said some. But, said others, giants live there! I love their description that they felt like grasshoppers alongside. Result: confusion and uproar.

I guess the Sinai desert wasn't the easiest place for the Israelites, but it was what they knew, it was where they'd found a self-identity, found faith, so moving beyond that may have all they desired, but also all they found disturbing.

The emergence into a new normality will be strange for us all, but it has to happen. Being able to visit loved ones and actually hug them will be a blessing for most. Churches gradually opening for worship is a joy. Being able to mix with groups of people will be a massive relief for the extroverts among us. But it also means we have to make decisions and pick up some of the difficult issues that have been on hold. The latest issue of "Private Eye" has a neat little cartoon with the caption, "Charming Picture of Child's Reunion with Grandmother After Lockdown" above a picture of Red Riding Hood by the bedside of the Wolf in Grandma's clothing. Reunions aren't always joyful! And then 'new normal' is a worrying term itself. Yet we have to move forward, there is no other option.

Perhaps Jesus' words in the Gospel reading set for this Sunday can help us. "Take my yoke upon you, and learn from me; for I am gentle and humble in heart, and you will find rest for your souls." (Matthew 11:29) It's a text I've sometimes struggled with, after frequently finding that walking with Jesus is a far from easy path that sometimes feels a bit heavy. But as we plough the new furrow ahead of us, we would be wise to yoke ourselves to Jesus rather than continue to struggle under our own heavy yoke of fear and distrust. Doing so does not mean that we'll avoid having to trudge through heavy stuff, but it does mean that the burden is eased by a calm; a peace that gives us a true strength. The burden is shared. And thereafter a rest that will fill our very self.

Very popular in Methodism is the Charles Wesley hymn, "Captain of Israel's host, and Guide' and I'd like to share the second and final verse with you:

By Thy unerring Spirit led,
We shall not in the desert stray;
We shall not full direction need,
Nor miss our providential way;
As far from danger as from fear,
While love, almighty love, is near.
Amen!

Road into the Sinai Desert

There are good things to look forward to – what might these be for you? There might be worrying things to deal with – what could these be for you? Pause for a moment, and bring these to God.

A prayer:

In an ever-changing world, Lord our God, our Father, we come to you, joyful at the changes that enlarge our vision and our very lives, yet hesitant at all that new situations bring to us.
Living Lord, comfort us all.

We bring those from whom we have been separated for what seems an age, families, friends, our church communities, thankful for all the means we have found of making connections yet sorrowful at the loss of close interaction – the handshake, the hug, the kiss.
Living Lord, hold us all.

We bring those who are charged with making decisions that affect all our lives, thankful for people of knowledge and thoughtfulness yet sorrowful at the divisions, the argument we hear, and sorrowful at the actions of those who disregard the safety of themselves and others.
Living Lord, guide us all.

We bring those affected by riot and violence, aware that in many corners of the world war and terror still dominate the lives of many innocents and that refugees still flee only to find themselves in new appalling, overcrowded, dangerous situations. Thankful for those who work to bring peace in families, communities and nations, we are sorrowful at the lack of awareness of our one-ness in your love.
Living Lord, bring your peace to all.

For ourselves, we pray that we might again take upon ourselves Jesus' yoke, so that, joined close to him, we may joyfully navigate the future, whatever it may bring.

We ask it in His name.
Amen

It's the little things that matter

The Gospel reading set for this Sunday is the Parable of the Sower, (Matthew 13: 1-9, 18-23) in which the sower goes out, manually scattering the seed in the time-honoured fashion. Much seed is lost: some shrivels on the path, some is taken by the birds, some roots only for the new growth to burn in the sun for lack of moisture in the thin soil.

It's a familiar story, often used at harvest-time, but my own thoughts were led towards the little things that help the crop to grow; the foundation layer, if you like.

First of all the soil, which must be cared for and not over-worked so that it is exhausted of nutrients; apparently improving the quality of soil has a good effect in counteracting global warming. Then come the myriad tiny creatures that work with the plants to enable growth. Even the munching creatures treating your plants as a restaurant have their own part to play. Honestly!

We like butterflies and most of us are alright with bees, but when it comes to the rather ugly bugs, a shriek and shudder is our first response, followed by death to the beastie. Now I freely admit to much shrieking and shuddering when I was younger, but even I have learned to admire and, in the case of bumblebees, to love them. All these creatures, small in size, make an immeasurable and unnoticed contribution to the life of this planet.

During Lockdown, many people have become aware of the wonder of the small things of earth. Several folk have told me of the 'loads' of bees they've seen this year – I think it probably has been a good year for bees, given our mild spring, but I suspect that in taking life more slowly, people are just noticing more and that's great. God places us in a wonderful world, and pausing to enjoy it and help it flourish is an important part of our calling and a great blessing. There was a children's hymn that went, "God bless the grass that grows through the cracks," – those little bits of greenery amongst the concrete slabs of the pavement. The little gifts of growth even in unlikely places.

But already, the roads are nearly as busy as before and lives are speeding up too. The Prime Minister tells us the future will be a case of "build, build, build," and while I am aware that people need homes and jobs, I know this will mean that more of the earth is covered over.

It's the little things that matter, not only the small creatures and people, but the little times we take to appreciate the wonder of creation and praise God for it all; the little steps we take to tend the earth and all that is within it, plants and creatures, for God loves it all.

"Consider the lilies of the field, how they grow; they neither toil nor spin, yet I tell you, even Solomon in all his glory was not clothed like one of these."
(Matthew 6: 28)

I pray that we continue to love and care and pray for the little things of earth.

Seed head of Goat's Beard or Jack-go-to-bed-at-noon

If you're interested, *The Garden Jungle, or Gardening to Save the Planet* by Dave Goulson is excellent in showing the place each creature has. He has a light, readable style – recommended!

And it's the often under-valued people who are essential. The insignificant in the world's eyes matter to God. Do you feel small and undervalued? God still loves you!

A prayer:

> Loving God and Father, this Lockdown has given us time and space to notice the detail of creation, and to remember the part played by the least and apparently insignificant in the health of the earth.
>
> We praise you for the wonder of creation, for the balance, the co-dependence, and for our own dependence upon you, who loves and cares for all you have made.

Jesus, loving Son of the Father, you taught us that the lowly and often overlooked are seen by you and loved. We remember with thanksgiving the huge part that the lowly paid and often scorned have to play in the health of the world.

We thank you for all those who work within our hospitals, care homes and in the community, caring for others often at risk to themselves, and for those who work within laboratories, running tests, seeking truth, seeking health for all people.
And in sorrow we bring those in turbulent parts of the world, where the onset of COVID-19 comes on top of many other pains and stresses – violence, war, poverty. We bring those crowded into slums, into refugee camps, into districts and lands where communities have been driven through loss of their own land, all places where the concept of social distancing is a bad joke. We seek blessing, and hope.

Loving Holy Spirit of God, you bring wisdom and insight to small and great alike. We pray the gift of your wisdom for those in places of government, at home and abroad, that they might hear the voice of the weak and powerless and find your compassion, your insight, painful though it may be.

And for ourselves, we ask eyes open to the glory of the world around us, to the glory that shines from so many lives, to the glory of our own creative gifts. May we use those gifts for the wellbeing of the earth, the wellbeing of great and small.
Thank you, Lord, for our one-ness with that same earth and for the part you need us to play through our prayers, our actions and our words, for the health of all.

To you, Lord God, Father, Son and Spirit, one in perfect unity, we offer our prayer. Amen

Chalk squealing down a blackboard... Sour fruit...

Puts your Teeth on Edge

Jeremiah 31: 27-34
John 9: 1-12
Mark 8: 22-26

'In those days they shall no longer say, "The parents have eaten sour grapes and the children's teeth are set on edge." '

(Jeremiah 31:29)

If ever there was a time for teeth to be on edge, I think this is it. Certainly, many people are edgy, and little annoyances seem huge. This is surely natural: we are living at a time when there is massive uncertainty. Increasingly aware that life as we have always known it may not be restored exactly as before, we are unsettled, in a sense like people who are mourning a loss. Our loss? Life as it was pre-COVID. And, inevitably, we start to look around to blame someone. Confidence in leadership is low: mixed messages, the sense that rules apply unevenly, the u-turns. It's right to admit when you're wrong and need to start again, no problem there, but perhaps there's also a need to admit from the outset that we are in uncharted territory and any decision has to be provisional. A bit of honesty rarely goes amiss.

So to the Gospel passages, both about healing of blindness. In John's Gospel, physical blindness is also a metaphor for spiritual blindness and maybe today we can also see it as a metaphor for lack of insight. Here, Jesus begins by refusing to play the blame game – who sinned? No-one, but in this situation, God's healing power can be shown. Jesus takes ordinary dust, dust from which, scripture says, we are made, and with his own spittle to make a paste which he places on the man's eyes. And he can see. With Jesus' help, the ordinary can become a means of healing.

In Mark's story, Jesus uses spittle and lays his hands on the man's eyes, but he can't see at first. Not clearly. He can discern that there are people around him, but they are shapeless, they look like trees, walking - so they must be people, walking not being a characteristic of your average tree. I believe that we are at that stage in our life as citizens and as members of the Church. We look around and kind of see, but not clearly, and that's an unhappy place to be: think of how you feel when you wake suddenly from a nap, disorientated. Where am I? Maybe even, who am I?

Jesus has to repeat the process for the blind man and the man himself has to look hard before he can see clearly. To see our way forward, I believe we need to stop dwelling in dark thoughts of blame, and seek the healing Jesus can bring to our lives and world. We turn again and again to prayer and to sharing our thoughts with trusted others so that we allow the Holy Spirit to bring us to a fuller insight of our way forward in our social and political life and in our life as the Church. We pray for strength to look hard with real vision, with insight, with the true wisdom of the Holy Spirit.

And we pray healing from that edginess!

Jeremiah goes on to tell his hearers that each bears their own responsibility for their lives. How we live our lives matters in terms of our interaction with our families, friends, neighbours and the people we meet casually in the street or shops. Do we live so that people are pleased to see us for all the right reasons? Do we live hopeful but realistic lives?

"Be the change you want to see in the world."
(Mahatma Gandhi)

A prayer:

Vision, insight, wisdom. Eternal, living Lord God, as we seemingly thrash about, uncertain, we pause for a moment to rest within your constant goodness, love and calm. Jesus promised he would never leave us: his risen presence remains, a support, a strength, and we know this with our heads, but sometimes find it hard to believe with our hearts when all around us seems shifting and uncertain. Forgive our needless fears, we pray.

Lord, all vision is yours; you see beyond and within. By your Spirit, guide our vision as we look out at the world. At the mess we have made of so much of nature; the poverty of so many, the wealth of the few.

We pray for those who are less afraid of COVID-19 than of hunger; those in nations for whom closure of schools means that their children go hungry and for whom Lockdown closes access to food. Strengthen, we pray, those who seek to bring aid to the thousands suffering thus, and open the eyes of the wealthy to see the difference their money might make.

Lord, all insight is yours; you understand, beyond and within. By your Spirit, guide those who study the current situation, and postulate ways forward. We pray for scientists, doctors and all medical staff, health officials, that they may be guided in their research to formulate safe and compassionate ways forward.

We pray, too, for those dealing with the mental effects of COVID-19 and Lockdown, that they may be granted insight into the lives of those they meet, and practical compassion. Lord, all wisdom is yours; a wisdom that extends from greatest to least. By your Spirit, guide those who have great decisions to make, ones affecting many.

We pray for governments of nations throughout the world, that they may seek ways of peace and cooperation for the good of all, rich and poor.

These prayers we offer in Jesus' name.
Amen

Being Masked

Wearing a mask is a big point of debate at the moment. Most of us accept the necessity of mask-wearing, uncomfortable though they may be, and much as they add to the washing, because it's important we wear them for the protection of others as well as ourselves.

Some people worry how we can show care for others when we're wearing a mask and our smile is hidden, but the truth is that we can see an expression through the person's eyes. I'm sure we've all had the experience of someone smiling at us, but while their mouth is in the shape of a smile, their eyes are betraying anger, indifference or even real hate.

We can certainly see an expression in someone's eyes. Unless we're solid with botox, the skin around our eyes creases when we smile. And eyes are expressive of joy or sadness; they can sparkle and they can be cold and quite frightening. Children who are abused often have wary eyes. Truthfully, the inner person shines through the eyes; our eyes reveal more than we think.

But what about the other kind of mask, the 'masks' we all of us wear?

The 'mask' of pretence that all is well or all is wrong. The 'mask' of pretence that I can cope when I know I'm falling to pieces. The 'mask' of pretending knowledge when we're really thrashing about, confused like everyone else. The 'mask' we wear to make people like us. Such masks – and there are as many as there are people – are sometimes needed, as in a crisis when we have to hold ourselves together; but worn regularly they don't bring health and can be hard to remove.

In the Bible, we read that Moses wore a face-covering when he came down Mount Sinai from meeting with God, because his face shone with such a radiance that people couldn't cope with it (Exodus 34:29-35). I suspect that the radiance, the love and strength of God cut through their 'masks' to reveal to them the people they really were, and it scared them. So, to avoid disturbing them, Moses went masked.

Jesus didn't. People looked on his face and found challenge, yes, but also openness and healing for their bruised souls, if they would accept it. In Mark 10:17-22 we have the story of a rich young man who came to Jesus, a genuinely devout man seeking eternal life. Jesus "looking at him, loved him." But the young man held onto his mask of wealth and status: he dared not let it go.

A question for us all – do I feel I have to hide who I really am?

And for us all to remember - God loves us behind our mask. Others will like knowing us too!

Here, on the upper reaches of Mount Sinai, where thousands had gone before me through the centuries, seeking God, I found my own cleft in the rock and sat in the silence, looking at this scene and reflecting on the story of Moses wishing to see God's face but being allowed to see only his back

(Exodus 33:18-23). Surely God will show us as much or as little of the shining light of his love as we need or can deal with at this moment.

A prayer:

Eternal, living Lord God, Father of all, we praise and bless you for the love that watches over us even when we are unaware and preferring to hide away behind our 'masks' of self-sufficiency.

Especially we praise and bless you for the love that sent Jesus to show us a life without pretence, a life open to love and to hurt; to accepting saint and sinner and bringing to both the healing and the new beginning they needed.

Lord, it is hard, to slip from behind our own masks. We have our ambitions, not for glory – well, in honesty, maybe for just a bit of glory, nothing too much – but to be the kind of person you want us to be, Christlike in our compassion, Spirit-led in our wisdom. We fall far short. And it's then we want to hide away, to pretend to others.

Eternal Father, your light and love penetrate our masks. Before you, we lay them down. Forgive us our sins and faults, we pray. Strengthen us by your Spirit to face the world with open eyes and hearts, to receive and to give your peace.

We bring, Loving Lord, the many people in the world today whose lives have been changed irrevocably because of the Lockdown: those who have lost loved ones, lost jobs, and those who fear loss to come, those whose financial security is weak, and those who care for seriously ill family and friends.

We bring those who are deeply disturbed by the uncertainties of the current moment and who, in their impotence, try to hit out at regulations. Bring peace of heart we pray.

And we bring those who have great power: the leaders of governments and of industry, that they may find the courage to be honest in their dealings with us all, to remember that we are fellow-citizens of the world, seeking the good of all; the good of the earth itself.

Our prayers we offer in the name of Jesus,
your Son our Saviour.
Amen

One Step at a Time

Matthew 14: 31-32
Psalm 150

As rules change, it's interesting to observe reactions. Going to our local Sainsburys, (making two journeys because, almost there, I realised I'd forgotten a mask – well, it increased the day's walk!) I was struck that people were being more observant of social distancing than had been the case only a few days before. Was it the masks being a constant reminder that the virus is still here?

Interesting, too, how people are resisting then embracing masks. Fashion houses have seized the moment, advertising whole outfits with matching masks. I confess I have indulged in rather upmarket masks. And transparent ones, to try out for preaching to help the listeners hear. (They didn't work!)

It's all a reminder that we are feeling our way and can only move forward in small steps.

Churches are reopening, but only where proper social distancing and cleaning and the rest can be maintained, and then only for shorter services with no singing. The no singing rule is tough, because singing has been part of worship through the ages: millennia ago people were singing and making music during their worship. Think how significant singing the Psalms has always been. Happily, music remains, whether recorded or played on the organ, piano or other instruments, to blend into and lift high our worship.

It's easy to see all this as a sad sign of how changed everything is, but can we see it instead as a little step forward? Because a little step forward is what it is.

Those of you who've made the crossing to Lindisfarne by foot, taking the Pilgrims' Way across the sand, will know how variable the terrain can be. Sometimes you can stride out over firm sand, but other times you have to tread lightly and carefully where it's wet and slippery, and sometimes you have to wade through quite deep water or into dark pools left by the retreating tide, placing your feet cautiously, unsure what lies within. Always, one step at a time.

The Pilgrim's Way is actually quite far, and the row of posts that mark it can seem endless. One of my companions when I walked St Cuthbert's Way in 2000 remarked afterwards that the poles seemed to stretch so far ahead, and the Island seemed to get no nearer, until he realised that here, as in life, the wise course was not to look ahead too often, but to concentrate on the here and now. Good advice for us today.

We take small steps, and live fully in the here and now. The mustard tree of Jesus' parable didn't leap overnight from seed to full maturity, home to the birds. It grew gradually, slowly, gently, with spurts of growth as the weather helped or hindered it. But it got there, and so will we, slowly, gradually, step by step.

The way ahead may be clear or might look extremely hard. May Jesus walk before us, with us always, a step at a time.

A prayer:

Loving, living Lord God, our Father, life can seem very confusing. We take steps forward yet fear that we may have to back-track and our progress is spasmodic. Like the goats in the picture, we are hesitant, for we might stumble and fall. We stumble so often. Forgive us, we pray, when our over-confidence in our own abilities leads us to barge ahead when we should pause and consider. Forgive us, we pray, when we hesitate too long, and lose our way. Remind us, we pray, that the Holy Spirit is with us always, to give us the wisdom we need in this and every moment of our lives, and that what may appear to be a minute step forward is just that, a positive progression along the way.

There are things we miss in our current situation. We miss the hymns we sing, the music that lifts our hearts and enriches our praise in worship. We bring before you, Lord, musicians composing, practising, finding ways of making music together through Zoom and other online means, seeking your blessing upon their honing of their craft and longing for the day their gifts can be shared in joyful outpouring. We give thanks for the time people have had to enjoy creation; to notice the trees and flowers, to observe the growth that continues, steadily, from seed to tender plant, to sturdy bush and tree. Help us to see in this the parable Jesus told, that from tiny beginnings great growth may come.

We pray for those people who are seeking answers, seeking comfort, seeking healing and peace, for those people who walk past our churches and wonder if there will be answers for them there. We ask your blessing upon them, and the gift of your Spirit to guide them to find or rediscover faith. May the love of Christ fill the thinking and deciding of the powerful and powerless, a love for all people, great and small. May that love be within us. We ask it in his name. Amen

Tossed about

Matthew 14: 22-36

© Helen E Gordon

A rough sea is beautiful to watch, but less so to sail, even in a modern ship. I have only been at sea once in a storm, a force eight, crossing from Bodo on the Norwegian coast to the Lofoten Islands in autumn, earlier than such storms normally blow up. I lay on my bunk in the darkness of night, glad to know that the Captain was an older man who, I told myself, would be well used to such conditions. Of course, we made the crossing safely, and back. It was only later that I discovered that there had been an earlier change of Captain, and the crossing had been the responsibility of a young man! An extremely capable one, of course.

For the disciples facing a headwind and rough seas, they were both Captain and crew. No time to imagine their lives in safe hands; their lives were in their own hands! And Jesus was on the shore.

In the other storm story, the story of Jesus stilling the storm, (Mark 4:35-41) Jesus was actually with them; they could yell at him, "Don't you care we're drowning?" No such luxury now.

I do wonder, thinking about the story, whether part of the problem was that there were too many captains on board. The disciples included four men from two fishing families and it could well be that there was disagreement on the way to handle the boat; who, I wonder, was in charge? Peter? Maybe, but he went overboard in all senses of the word when he saw Jesus and left the rest to handle the ship, which wouldn't have impressed me if I'd been James or John, left to struggle against the wind with the added possibility of having to hook him out of the water.

Just at this moment, we may feel that we are 'all at sea,' and a stormy one at that. With so many changes happening and so many conflicting views of how to go forward, the image of the choppy sea certainly matches the way we seem to be tossed this way and that, news battering us like so many waves. The image falls down there, because the disciples were on a sea they knew: we are in uncharted territory and largely because of that, for many people there is an unease with leadership. Do they know what they're doing? Who do we believe?

But the part of the story that particularly strikes me in relation to ourselves, is that Jesus came out to the boat walking across the stormy water. He didn't silence the storm, as in the other storm story; the waves didn't subside and the wind didn't drop until he was on board with them. I think there's a lovely image there for us here and now. No matter how awful the present moment may be and how uncertain the future may seem, Jesus is out there among the chaos and the uncertainty, like a lighthouse as the waves crash around it. But unlike a light, Jesus is not fixed, but moving across the chaos, coming to us to bring his own peace. Let him on board!

The prayer of the Breton fishermen comes to mind: "O God, your sea is so great and my boat is so small," and thinking of which, perhaps we can pray, "O God, this life is so complicated and my courage is so weak."

A prayer:

Eternal Lord God, Father of all, at the moment of creation, your Spirit hovered across the chaos on soft wings, bringing peace from disorder. Your Son, Jesus, walking over the chaos of the sea, brought peace to frightened disciples. Always, always, Lord, you watch over us and in Jesus come to us when we are afraid and lost; your Spirit touches our lives with the same wings of calm that brought order from primal chaos.

Eternal Lord God, Father of all, we are awed by the depth of your love for us. Confident in that love, we come to you with much upon our hearts and minds. We think of those charged with leadership at this time – governments, our own and throughout the world, asking the guidance of the Holy Spirit.

Lord, we pray for an honesty and openness to bring on board all people so that we understand what is asked of us, and the true depth of the problems ahead; so that we can think and pray with clarity and find common purpose.

We remember, too, that the Lockdown filling our news and thoughts has enabled other, important news to slip out of sight. Lord, bring help to those who are suffering under unjust regimes, through oppression.

As many of our churches reopen, we ask your guidance and blessing, for the reopening is of itself difficult; different. We face one another, masked. We are seated apart. The conviviality of coffee after service is gone.

Yet, Lord, you are there. The presence of Jesus among us encourages us. Your Spirit comforts and enlivens us. We sing within our hearts, and one day, we will sing loud praises again! Until then, we offer our prayers in Jesus' name, he who is with us always. Amen

Whose Fault?

© Helen E Gordon

Luke 12:54-13:9

When things go wrong, we want to know who to blame. Could nations have dealt better with Coronavirus? What or who was at fault in the explosion and loss of life in Beirut?

There's nothing new about this, because humans seem to like to have reasons why things have happened and to be able to apportion blame; indeed it was an issue with which Jesus dealt.

In the above passage from Luke's Gospel, we read of a couple of nasty disasters: the slaughter of some Galileans by the Romans and the fall of the tower of Siloam which killed eighteen people (Luke 13:1-4), and people were wondering whether those thus killed had done something bad to bring disaster upon their heads, literally, in the case of the tower collapse. Oh, come on, says Jesus, were they any worse than all the people not killed? Clearly not.

The eighteen people on whom the tower collapsed were presumably just in the wrong place at the wrong time; it was chance. But most people don't like chance: it makes us nervous because it takes away our sense of control. Much easier when there is someone to blame. Well, in this case there might have been: the jerry-builders of Siloam, perhaps?

At this moment, when we look at the circumstances of the explosion in Beirut, we are shown a line of blame, of bad decisions and of casual disregard. Of corruption. If we look at the circumstances of the spread of Coronavirus, there are lines of blame, of bad decisions, of casual disregard. Of corruption?

Corruption, casual disregard could have been behind the slaughter of the Galilean pilgrims come to Jerusalem to make their Temple sacrifice. Were these people freedom-fighters from the north? Or innocent casualties of Roman edginess? We don't know, because sometimes it is easy to see who is at fault, but other times it's harder to decide. But beneath so much disaster is a selfishness, a care for 'me' rather than 'us' that puts the 'us' at risk.

So, what about thee and me? The end of Luke 12 has been about watching out, feeling the atmosphere, knowing, in the deepest sense of the word, the present time. And knowing our own responsibility. It's fine pointing at the other, but what about our own fault? Are we good at admitting when we've made a mistake and asking pardon? Or, like children, do we cry, "I didn't do it!" "It's me!" or "But I was only just . . . "

I remember the film Love Story, with its line, "Love means never having to say you're sorry," when the truth (as any married couple can attest) is that love means constantly having to say sorry, and it's only as and when all ordinary people can take that grown-up responsibility of saying, "I was at fault. Forgive me. Let's put it right," that the world can begin to change.

Can we learn to admit when we are at fault, to be honest with one another and live in harmony? Of course we can! May Jesus guide and bless us all.

A prayer:

Loving God and Father, we look out at the world you have given into our care, and we see great beauty, great wonder. Along with the beauty of creation we see the beauty of love shown in the small acts of caring, the small words of comfort, the gentle, "I'm sorry."

We see the wonder of creation, the wide sweep of the landscape, the depth of sky, and the wonder of love that forgives and forgives again. Thank you, Lord, that it is the beauty and wonder of your love that is reflected in our own loves, in our own lives.

But as we look out at the world, we see, along with the beauty and love, great pain. We bring the citizens of Beirut at this terrible time: those who mourn loved ones, those whose homes and livelihoods have been destroyed in an instant, those who are left shocked and traumatised: victims and rescue workers alike.

We bring too, the anger and the blame that follows all such disasters. Lord, may your Spirit enter within the debate and the thinking to guide along right pathways that will lead to peace and not strife, that will lead to rebuilding of homes and lives and not to festering discord.

We remember, too, that Lebanon has been the destination of many refugees for many years, and we ask for them peace and hope. Their pain and loss we hold, and offer to you, our God and Father, through Jesus, who gave his life for all, for the little and least and the rich and powerful.

We pray a spirit of honesty within the corridors of power, a willingness to admit to fault, to seek forgiveness; a willingness to seek new ways of working together.

And within local communities, may people live with an awareness of the needs of others, live with a regard for the safety of all.

May your Holy Spirit guide all our thinking into ways of justice and of peace for all people; help us look, reflect, listen . . . then speak and act in ways that will lead forward into your kingdom alone.

Bless we pray, those who share with us these prayers and those we hold in our hearts, as we offer them in Jesus' name, your Son, our Saviour.

Amen

Joyful Inside

© Helen E Gordon

A sense of joy deep inside, no matter what's happening, can be a great gift. A hugely popular film clip is the sequence in "Singing in the Rain" in which Gene Kelly dances along the street amid a downpour. Apart from the energy and skill of the dance, the sheer exuberant joy expressed lifts our hearts, no matter how many times we may see it.

But dance is a particularly good medium for expressing inner feelings. In the ballet version of Charles Dickens' *A Christmas Carol*, dance very much represents the inner world of the characters: Bob Cratchit breaks away from his desk to dance fluently, revealing the joyful inner self normally crushed by his employer, Scrooge. We see Scrooge himself, as a young man, dancing – but the older man dances not a step, his movements sharp and tight; though when he wakes on Christmas Day knowing redemption, well! Then he dances, can hardly keep his feet still, except when he is standing on the sidelines, smiling at the joy of others.

I suspect St Paul had this inner joy. Before his dramatic meeting with the risen Christ on the road to Damascus, he was a driven, angry man, secure in his high status. After that meeting he lost the safety of his status as a card-carrying Pharisee, and faced tremendous dangers and humiliations – the list he shares in 2 Corinthians 11: 1-31 is pretty daunting, but he coped, I believe, through that inner strength he had; that inner knowledge of being called and loved by Christ. It shines through that lovely passage in Romans 8 (Romans 8: 31-39), the certainty that nothing can separate us from the love of God through Christ Jesus.

An inner joy is not just being happy all the time or always seeing the bright side - that can really get on other people's nerves and is more likely to win you a black eye than eternal peace!

The Jesuit Gerald O'Mahoney expresses it very well as being a 'still point' which we all have, but sense only fleetingly, and to maintain it we have to push against our own tendencies to gloom and depression on the one side and over-elation on the other.[1] This still point, an inner joy, is where we are completely ourselves as God made us to be and where we function best; where, like Scrooge on Christmas Day, we can look at the people around us and rejoice for them.

From this point of stillness/joy, we can cope with all that is thrown at us by life. I'm not saying we don't struggle, because we do, I'm not saying we don't despair, because we do – but we don't stay in those states. That inner joy will hold us, and I fear that we're going to need to cultivate that inner peace and joy because, while not wishing to depress anyone, it looks as if the future is not going to be easy for any of us.

In Singing in the Rain, truth wins through. The talented heroine is recognised, and the shrill-voiced 'star' exposed as a fraud. Inner joy brings truth to bear for everyone! Worth cultivating it!

Be quietly at peace with yourself so that you can face whatever life brings.

---

1   Gerald O'Mahony *Finding the Still Point* (Exploring Prayer Series) 1993 Eagle

A smile or a frown – which are you wearing at this moment? Does a smile or frown represent you as you look at the future? Which most represents you as you look around at the people you see in the street or on television? In truth, it's fine to be either, at any one time!

But do we seek that knowledge of God's love for each of us that lets us be unhappy sometimes and happy other times without being overcome? God does love you. Always.

A prayer:

> Eternal, living Lord God our Father, thank you, thank you for your love for each one of us, for each one sharing in these thoughts and prayers and for all your children, near and far.
>
> Forgive us when we either take this love for granted or doubt it's there at all. Forgive us when we decide that we can do all things in our own strength; when we struggle along and blame ourselves when we fail.
>
> Forgive us, we pray, our weaknesses and the faults that are clear to everyone, and those only you see, so that, forgiven, we might glow with an inner joy that helps us see ourselves and others through the eyes of your love alone.
>
> Remembering your great love, we pray for those who have little or no experience of love. Those many children brought up in households where there is a chilliness of spirit, where arguments abound or where there is violence, physical or mental, that crushes the person within.
>
> Lord, we pray your healing into those situations and the guiding of your Spirit to bring alongside both child and adult others who will accept them for who they are - your beloved children - and help rebuild shattered lives.

We bring people who, today, are going through terrible suffering – those imprisoned for their faith or for protesting on behalf of the poor, their families, not knowing how or where they are. For them we pray that inner core of strength to hold them and to tell them that they are not alone, that others remember them and pray for them; weep with them.

We bring people who, today, look to the future with fear: those who have lost their employment and who fear losing their home too, those who have lost loved ones and see only a bleak future ahead, those who are just plain scared because nothing is normal. Lord Jesus, enfold them, we pray, in your love; may your arms wrap around them warmly, and may the Holy Spirit motivate, we pray, those in power to truly seek the wisdom to plan for the good of all people.

We ask it in the name of Jesus, who gave his life that all may have life in all its fullness.

Amen

Dreaming

During Lockdown, many people found they were dreaming and remembering their dreams, whereas before they either thought they didn't dream (unlikely) or could never remember the dream (likely). Nighttime dreams can be weird, or frightening, or comforting, but they seem to be ways of sorting out our thoughts that are necessary to our brain's health.

In a strange way, we sometimes feel that the Lockdown is a kind of dream from which we hope we'll wake up soon, and everything will be as it was. But rather than fretting, we can use this time to pray for a vision of what can be, for dreams can be visions that inspire us.

The Bible has many instances of God using dreams or visions to guide (eg. Joseph, Matthew 1:19-25, Joseph and the Wise Men, Matthew 2:12-15) and also to challenge; Peter's dream and subsequent understanding that verified the Gentile Mission (Acts 10:9-48) is an example. And, of course, there is the Old Testament Joseph, there are the Prophets – so many dreamers, so many visionaries!

But in all of these instances, the vision or dream required to be acted upon.

We all have day-dreams in our youth; then, as we get older, we also have dreams for the young in our families. Most of us have dreams for society. The reality, of course, is that many of these dreams turn to dust and it's just as well that some of them do! The sadness lies in the dreams that do not match our capabilities. Were I to dream of being a great mathematician, for example, I would be doomed to disappointment, even if I worked very hard. We need to be real!

Dangerous dreams are those of personal glory at all costs, and I leave you to provide your own examples of this from the world today. There are plenty to choose from.

I go back to the fact that God uses our dreaming to share visions of what can be, but those dreams, those visions require action on our behalf. Fulfilment of the dream of using our natural abilities requires that we actually use them rather than just dreaming what could be 'if'. Fulfilment of the dream of a just world requires us to act justly in our own lives and to speak out against injustice, even when we're a bit scared to do so. And all of it needs a whole lot of prayer.

Iona Abbey (picture overleaf), was restored following George MacLeod's vision of the ruin made new, but it took a great deal of faith, prayer, courage and sheer hard work before the dream became a reality, and all that has been needed subsequently to maintain the Iona Community and to seek further vision. But the result has been massive blessing for thousands who have travelled to the island and found a depth to their faith and new life. What are your deepest dreams? Will you work and pray to make them new?

Pray that we all dream dreams of hope for everyone and work to make the vision live.

Iona Abbey in June.
Both photographs Ruth Crofton, who loves skies!

A prayer:

Loving God, who weaves our dreams into things of wonder, through them calling us, guiding us, laughing with us, we praise and thank you for the gift of imagination, of daydreaming that leads to vision and hope, and the playful dream that brings us peace.

In this confusing time in the life of the world, we pray your Spirit's gentle guiding: the breeze that blows our thoughts in right directions and towards goals that will liberate the earth and bring peace to all; the breeze that blows through the dusty corridors of power to bring a breath of life to stifling thoughts and decisions.

In this nightmare time for so many who are afflicted by violence and fear all around them and the danger of COVID-19 always present, we pray the healing touch of your Spirit, within nations at war, within refugee camps, within ruined cities and devastated countryside, bringing hope where there is despair, trust where it is broken, healing where there is illness and pain and loss . . .

In this gentle, dreaming time, when many have time to pause and look about them, we pray the discernment of your Spirit to see what is and what is not of you, and to choose the right, the life-giving, way forward.

Bring light, we pray, to churches emerging into new ways of worship; bring true vision of what can be now and what could be in the future.

Loving God, Father, Son and Spirit, to you we offer our praying, our dreaming, our living, that they may be used for the furtherance of your Kingdom of justice and of peace.

We ask it in Jesus' name.
Amen

New Beginnings

Dawn, Sharm el Sheikh

Children returning to school, people encouraged to go back to work, churches reopening - is this a time of new beginning?

As a child at the start of a new school year, I loved all the new exercise books, with that special paper-smell and their spotless pages. I don't think I was alone in making a resolution to keep the books special: neat, free of crossings-out and blots (I am old enough to remember pens you dipped in ink!). And if we didn't think it ourselves, the teacher suggested the idea, forcefully. How long did the resolution last? I don't know about you, but in my own case not long at all, but then the tension of trying to do my very, very best writing somehow seized up my hand and it became almost my worst writing . . . honestly!

Much as we long for it, a new beginning can never be fully that, because we bring ourselves to it, with all our imperfections. Our past influences our present and our future.

So, as churches reopen with services foreshortened, bereft of singing and with no coffee and chat afterwards, how do we handle it?

One option is to look back and think only of what is not. This was something the Israelites, led by Moses across the wilderness majored in until Moses was ready to give up on them (Exodus 11:15). Then subsequently, when in exile, there was more looking back: "On the willows there we hung up our harps ... how could we sing the Lord's song in a foreign land?" (Psalm 137)

We have a choice. Do we think only of what is not, or do we draw on the riches of the past and adapt them to the present moment? Bereft of singing, a decision was made in one congregation to hum, on the basis that you hum with closed mouth, and it's actually very beautiful. We can embrace the chance to be quiet, together. To listen to new music, whether recorded or live. We can experiment, within the set parameters, and praise God in new ways that connect with the old.

Jesus tackled this issue when he spoke about seeking the kingdom of God (Matthew 13:44-52). "Every scribe who is trained for the kingdom of heaven is like the master of a household who draws out of his treasure what is new and what is old." As we move forward uncertainly, rather than sighing for the past we can draw on the old and the new to the glory of God and the building up of his kingdom here on earth.

And if there are one or two (or more!) blots and errors and wobbles along the way, don't worry. God knows our weaknesses and our strengths, and his Spirit will help us, and Christ will lead us, however uncertain the way may be.

Pause for a moment and reflect – What have you learnt from the past? How do you feel, today? How do you feel about the future? For the past - give thanks. For the present – live fully. For the future – trust.

Iona, Columba's bay where he landed c.563 to begin his new life, one that brought blessing to countless people.

A prayer:

Thankful we come to you, Eternal Lord God our Father, with thoughts of the past. There is so much that brings us joy in the remembering, and so much that brings us sorrow or even anger.

Some of this has shaped us for the good, and we praise and thank you for times that have not always been easy, but have taught us much about you, about the world and about ourselves.

Some memories remain dark within us, and we try to offer them to you now, asking that the light of Christ may shine within the dark, shadowy places of our lives to bring forgiveness, healing, peace and new hope.

Eyes wide open, we look at the world around us. We are in a strange place, Lord, where advice, instructions change day by day, a place in which the old certainties have been shaken.

Yet, you are with us still, no matter how uncertain the times,
and we praise and thank you for that truth, and for the blessing
we can draw from the past, as well as finding new blessing in the
future.

Thank you for those who are a blessing to us: those who
encourage us by their words and actions, and those who
faithfully hold us in their thoughts and prayers.

May we be such people for others, resting upon your strength.
Loving, Eternal God, Father, Son and Spirit,
we praise you, today and always.

Amen

On Hold

Many happy events have been deferred because of Coronavirus – weddings, big celebrations, holidays. The second picture is a sighing after my own deferred journey along the coast of Norway at Christmas! Next year? Perhaps.

During our lives, most, if not all of us, have had to delay various happenings. Couples waiting to get married until they can afford it; waiting to have a home of our own until we can afford it; saving for the big holiday – how often money drives our waiting! But what is different now? I think there are several aspects.

Firstly, think back to times when a week or fortnight's annual holiday was all there was, or when our first home contained a lot of second-hand furniture passed on to us - or fobbed off on us! Deferral of hopes was part of life, but for years now this hasn't been the case for many, with the advent of increased wealth and credit. Deferral comes hard now. Then, more significantly, there is the matter of choice – we ourselves may choose to delay an event for many reasons, but it is our own choice. These delays that are forced upon us have an altogether harsher feel. And then there is a general air of uncertainty – how long will this go on?

The phrase, "How long?" crops up in the Psalms of lament: how long must I suffer, how long until the wicked get their just desserts, how long are the people to suffer under the heel of the oppressor? How long? And we ask, how long are the people to suffer under the constrictions of the Lockdown, and answer is there none.

And then, of course, there are the delays to medical procedures and this particular delay brings great pain and stress to add to the overall worries.

Let's look at St. Paul. In his letter to the Philippians, he speaks of his own circumstances in prison, and of the ways in which his imprisonment has actually aided the spread of the Gospel. The imperial guard is now aware of the Gospel, and his situation has actually made his fellow Christians bolder in speaking out (Philippians 1: 12-18). Then comes a very positive statement.

Paul will continue to rejoice – rejoice, even though his plans and dreams have been put on hold. Whatever happens to him, whether he lives or dies, Christ will be exalted. Paul approaches death with equanimity: "Living is Christ and dying is gain." In fact, he wants to be with Christ in death, which is not the cry of the terminally depressed but a straightforward statement that when it's time, he's ready. In the meanwhile, he is content to remain for the people he is encouraging in faith and in joy. (Philippians 1:18b-26)

I find this a great word for the present moment. Whatever is to come and whatever our circumstances now, we can live our lives in a way that shows the Gospel in our finding of the contentment to be exactly where we are, for what we can do and be here and now.

Pause for a moment. What have you had to delay or lose because of the Lockdown? If the issue is a hard one, let yourself grieve the loss, but also let Christ put his arms around you to comfort you.

Read Matthew 23: 37b

A prayer:

At this time of great uncertainty, of delay and disappointment, we come before you, Eternal God, who was and is and is to come, whose presence in Christ is with us always, no matter what the circumstances of our lives. We thank you for that presence, that strength upon which we can rest secure, and for the guiding and comfort of your Spirit, with us always.

In an uncertain time in our own nation, we pray for those tasked with making decisions that affect us all now and in the future. May they be guided by your Holy Spirit to pause and reflect on how these decisions will affect the poorest in society.

Lord, bring wisdom and compassion in all decision-making we earnestly pray. In the world are many people suffering crippling uncertainty – of employment and of finance, of housing, food and drink and of delays of many kinds. We bring those worrying at the delay of medical procedures and those who are ill or in any kind of distress, that they might find healing of body and spirit. We bring those fretting at the delay of weddings, of moving house, of longed-for meetings with family and friends and longed-for holidays. Hold them, we pray in this present moment, bring a calming of anxiety, and acceptance of the joy and the potential of the here and now, and the continued looking forward to what can be.

As we rejoice in the ongoing reopening of churches for worship, we bring those fellowships who have had to delay reopening, or who are reopening with a sense of trepidation, that they may find renewed blessing in being together, in shared prayer, in peace. Help us all, wherever we are, find joy and hope in this present moment so that, strengthened, we can face whatever delays and uncertainties await us in the future.

We ask it in Jesus' name, he who gave his life
that all may have life in its fullness.
Amen

Game of Snakes and Ladders, anyone?

If you're competitive, it's a tense game, is Snakes and Ladders. The toss of the dice, the small ladder giving us a lift . . .the big ladder hurtling us up towards the finish line . . . the little snake, sneaking us back a row or two . . . the big snake, sliding us right back down.

We seem to be getting somewhere with the Lockdown, then down we go again . . . just like a game of snakes and ladders? The ladder of increased freedom which brings us joy, not only in that we can meet up with others but in the knowledge that we are edging up towards the time we will be quite free of the virus . . . and then the slide back down to restrictions, some of which we find it hard to understand. A bit arbitrary, like Snakes and Ladders.

The concept of chance is a tricky one. I'm aware that many Christians believe that God has our lives all mapped out while others, myself included, believe that there is a randomness in life that we all face and it's how we respond to that randomness which matters, that God strengthens and guides us through the tough times that fall to us. I don't choose to go into detail, but please be assured I don't speak in a vacuum but have much experience of loss and both mental and physical ill health. But, hey, I'm mostly happy. Well, sometimes more than others!

Faith is not an insurance policy, nor are we in a game, passive counters being moved about at the throw of a dice. We may find ourselves in difficult situations, as at the present time, but we have choice in how we live life: we can live selfishly, or we can live with an awareness of the needs of others. We can live as if our little corner of the earth is all there is, or we can live knowing that there is something precious and beautiful around, within and beyond. The glory of creation; the blessing of others; the life and love of God, Father, Son and Spirit.

St Paul understood this: he lists, in 2 Corinthians 11 a list of hardships that can make anyone gasp, but he continued to work for the sake of the people who sneered at him, and to rejoice that they might learn the truth of the Gospel of Christ. In Romans 12: 9-13 he teaches a way of living that reflects the love of Jesus: "Rejoice in hope, be patient in suffering, persevere in prayer."

Jesus himself warned his disciples that the way ahead of them was not going to be easy, that he was sending them out as lambs among wolves (Luke 10:1-3), warned them that they would have to take up their own cross if they were to follow him. (See Matthew 10:37-38, 16:24-26, Mark 8:34-37, Luke 9:23-25.) With so many references, I think we're meant to take this teaching very seriously and get on with living in the light of it.

The Lockdown is a big thing to face, made more difficult by the changing instructions we receive. We might be sliding down a snake at the moment, but we'll move on to find a ladder sooner or later and in the meanwhile surely we need to live so that all might live as full lives as possible, even within whatever restrictions are placed upon us.

Snakes and Ladders is a good game if you know how to laugh. Then the snakes are less important, can even be a source of fun. "Oh, down we go again! Whee!"

And don't forget, you need to put a bit of effort into climbing ladders!

A prayer:

Living, Eternal Lord God, we rejoice in hope, for you have placed us in this world, a place of beauty and wonder with signs all around us of new life, opportunity for new beginning, day by day.

We reach out joyfully for the hope you promise of life in its fullness, the life won for us by Jesus our Saviour, your Son, who did not avoid the suffering of Crucifixion: mockery and death, that we might be raised to life in you.

We praise and thank you, too, for the strengthening and guiding of your Holy Spirit to give us the energy and will to climb whatever steeps we need to face.

But patience, Lord, that is difficult. Suffering, loss, restrictions of many kinds come to us and we long to be rid of them.

We bring to you those who have had to cancel large events that matter to them, those still unable to meet with all their family, those who feel their lives unduly circumscribed. For them, Lord, we pray patience and calm.

But we also bring those whose lives are restricted without hope of swift change – those imprisoned, especially remembering those imprisoned for sharing their faith, or, in unjust regimes, for helping the poor.

We bring refugees and asylum seekers in their desperation . . . those who suffer natural disaster: wildfires, drought, flood, seismic activity.

Perseverance in prayer, Lord, can be difficult too. We persevere in remembering and thinking of others, but often we do not know how to pray, or our thoughts and words seem inadequate. Yet we remember that you know us and understand us better than we know ourselves and know the yearnings of our hearts.

We bring those situations and people that lie heavily upon our hearts and minds; we think of them, we think of you, knowing that you hold all in your love.

We bring those who persist in doing good, no matter the reversals they face, speaking out against injustice, even imperilling their own lives, speaking truth in the corridors of power, when that truth is not welcomed, alerting the world to climate change.

For all who speak out we ask the power of your Spirit to bring wisdom and the persistence to continue. Hold us, Lord God our Father, in your love. In Jesus' name we ask it.

Amen

Laugh, and the world laughs with you

Ella Wheeler Wilcox (1850-1919)

It might seem strange to focus on laughter when we're facing the possibility of another full Lockdown, but maybe that makes it even more appropriate. Sometimes I have been accused of finding everything funny, which is unfair: I take many things very seriously indeed, but my own way of coping with really bad situations – and I know I'm not alone in this – is to look out for the bizarre, the absurd in it all and laugh, and that truly helps me.

Many years ago I used to holiday at Scargill House in Yorkshire, their holiday weeks often attended by a lot of single people like myself. One free afternoon four of us decided to go for a walk, even though it was raining – persistent, penetrating drizzle. Being relative strangers, we shared stories as we walked. I had recently been widowed, another woman had been made redundant and, at her age, was unsure if she could find further employment. A third had been so pressured at work that she had had a breakdown. The fourth had a child with a rare medical condition, coping with which had broken her marriage and now she'd become ill herself. There was a bit of sharing of 'where is God in this', but mostly we listened quietly to one another.

Back indoors, we stood, dripping gently, then one of us – I can't remember who - said, "What a pathetic bunch to go for a walk together!" And we suddenly found the situation funny and laughed at ourselves, really laughed. (The dry people walking past looked at us as if we were plain crazy!) Afterwards the lady whose child was so ill said that she couldn't remember the last time she'd laughed like that, and how healing it had been.

I firmly believe that finding the funny side in a situation is not contrary to our calling as Christians. There is Humour in the Bible, probably more than we think, because we don't know all the situations in which people spoke, or their tone of voice. For instance, read Galatians 5: 1-14, part of Paul's rebuttal of the people who were insisting that men had to be circumcised before they could become Christians, and imagine the people hearing the letter read out - and chuckling, as they no doubt did (v.12), before they had the joy of being encouraged.

In the Old Testament, we have Elijah mightily sarcastic as the prophets of Baal tried to bring down fire (1 Kings 18: 26-27), but given that he was in a rather hyper mood he's perhaps not the best role model. My point, though, is that faith does not have to be a gloomy, serious matter, and that humour, finding the absurd, the foolish and laughing, should be part of our faith, especially when we're laughing at our own absurdities and, dare I say, noticing the absurdities of the church.

Finding humour, lightness in our present situation is not easy. Finding absurdity is easier – the ruling that pubs had to close at ten (to which I'm certainly not objecting) has got people laughing: does the virus only come out to play at ten o'clock? Sadly, though, the absurdity of much today is less funny than dangerous, and that has to be faced and challenged, that is the time to be serious.

But while there are times to be serious it is still possible to find a lightness of spirit and even to laugh, always.

Does God laugh? Well, he must have a sense of humour: after all, he made human beings and they really can be absurd! Definitely me. Maybe even you?

Live   Laugh   Love

Pause to think – who makes your life better? Who helps you laugh, and love?

A prayer:

Creator, creative Lord God, you have so placed us that we live in a world that is both beautiful and bizarre, a world in which we find depths of wonder and awe and depths of uncertainty, sorrow and pain. It can be hard to live through the pain and sorrow, hard to live with uncertainty, as at the present moment. We try to be positive for the sake of others, but it can be draining and leave us feeling low.

Father, your Son, Jesus, lived through a time of deep uncertainty too, lived with the knowledge of the death that would come to him. His early followers, too, lived with great uncertainty and, sometimes, great fear.

Loving Lord, when we are fearful, hold us tightly in your love, and by your Holy Spirit give us the courage we need with the guidance to know the wise way to live and the best way forward.

Bless, we pray, those who work to bring help in our own country and abroad,
* those who work within hospitals and clinics, and within people's homes;
* those who work in food banks;
* those who go into places and among people other folk fear and reject, bringing new hope and life, smiles, laughter and love;
* those who lead acts of worship that lift our hearts nearer to you and inspire us to live more fully each day.

Thank you for these people, and for those we meet who smile and laugh, even when they themselves are hurting; those who raise our spirits by their words and by their lives.

Help us, loving, living God to be people who bring hope and joy by just being ourselves. And when we are very preoccupied with who we are and all that is wrong, help us, next time we look in a mirror, to see our own absurdity, and laugh.

We ask it in the name of Jesus your Son, he who offers hope and joy to all.
Amen

"God did not send the Son into the world to condemn the world, but in order that the world might be saved through him."
John 3: 17

PS. I gave my own nieces a good laugh yesterday when they saw the scar from a small facial operation I recently had to have. "It looks as if you've had a face-lift!" they crowed.

PPS. I haven't.

The Patience of Creation

Nature is very patient. Plants reach maturity in their own time, buds, leaves, flowers, seeds develop and fall in their own time; they fall or spin away freely and wait to become covered by earth, wait for the cold that will split the hard protective shell of the seed. Then comes another wait in the cold of the earth for the right moment, that signal time for the seed to sprout and emerge into the early warmth of spring. None of this can be hurried; left to itself, each stage comes at the right time.

Many hundreds of years ago, people wouldn't have needed to be reminded of all this. Even in the cities, they were aware of the passing times and seasons, but in our modern world, when we can buy fruit grown on the other side of the world all year round (even if it doesn't taste exactly right) and where autumn leaves are only a slippery nuisance, we need reminding of the gradual nature of growth, especially at this time when we are facing a virus, a being of nature that needs to be studied and understood, against which trials must be carried out, learning through failure as well as success. Like the Psalmist, we want to cry, "How long, O Lord?" (Psalm 89: 46-49).

It's not knowing that's hard, isn't it? Not knowing how long it'll take for the infection rate to fall, how long to find a vaccine. This is the very hardest time to be patient and wait.

And patience is not always our forte. My mother, who was first to admit to impatience, late in life had a fridge magnet bearing the prayer: "Lord, grant me patience and grant it NOW!" and though this is a joke, there's a truth in it. We want to take a pill to cure our aches and pains, and if they continue, there must be a stronger pill. We want what we want, now – or soon. The calm of the writer of Ecclesiastes is not our calm (Ecclesiastes 3:1-8).

The humble horsechestnut can help us. For the child, the temptation is to knock them from the trees when they are bright green, like this, rather than the often rather tatty-looking specimens that have fallen to earth. Mistake. Cut open the softer specimens, and you get only a white, immature seed. It has to take time to grow, to fatten, to ripen. Even though the outer coat becomes hard, prickly, protected within is the inner seed slowly growing, maturing to the point when it can become a source of new life.

We get impatient sometimes, we're human. Even Jesus got impatient! (Luke 9: 41). But patience is indeed a virtue, and living authentically while we wait, praying for the God-given future which is growing unseen, maturing in quietness, can bring its own peace to our souls.

Nature may be patient - We find it rather harder!

Waiting for things to change – waiting for COVID-19 numbers to fall – waiting for a cure – for a vaccine – waiting for life to be normal . . . What do you most long for? Peace would be good. Are we willing to work and pray quietly, patiently that all creation might find real peace?

A prayer, adapted from Season of Creation, an ecumenical Celebration Guide.

Eternal God, Creator, Redeemer, Life-giver, one in perfect unity, you are a community of love reconciling all of creation, inspiring and renewing new life. We praise and bless you for the gift of the natural world; for all that it can teach us of patient growth to maturity.

We confess with sorrow our demand that the earth produce beyond its limits, produce all we want quickly, for we are in bondage to the desire for more. We confess that we easily think of creation as a given rather than a gift to be cherished. We confess our failure to share fairly what we receive from the earth. Forgive us, we pray. Place within us a peace of heart that will wait, with patience for the earth to renew itself and for your word to take root within our hearts.

Bring healing to all our lives, that we might sow beauty, not pollution and destruction. Touch the hearts of those who look only for gain at the expense of the poor and the earth, and lead them along new, peaceful and open ways of thinking and being.

At this time when there is so much fear, so much pressure to find cures, vaccines against COVID-19, we pray for scientists who work to research all this, asking for them the guidance of your Holy Spirit.

We bring to you all who work within the National Health Service, often much pressured by government and patients to do more, to achieve more. Especially, Lord, we bring to you all who are tasked with making decisions that affect us all: may your Holy Spirit breathe a word of wisdom and peace above the many competing voices, a word that brings calm, hope, healing.

We bring those who work the land, whether in huge farms or small gardens, that they may rejoice in their one-ness with creation, with the joys as well as the sadness, with the new life they foster as well as the losses they mourn.

In this season of autumn, help us, Lord, to look to the trees and plants, aware more of the potential new life in seeds and fruits, than of the dying-back. Like the trees, help us all rest in the patient quiet, awaiting the warmth of spring, of new beginning for all.

We ask it in the name of Jesus, who laid down his life to bring a new, vibrant beginning for each one.

Amen.

Frustration!

© Helen E Gordon

Many of us, today, are feeling frustrated, and when we're like that it's a good idea to look back at the roots of frustration. Look back to the time you were a toddler, throwing a tantrum – and just because time has laid a gentle blanket of forgetting over our earliest years, don't kid yourself. You too had tantrums. Why?

The toddler screams (and all the rest!) with frustration when prevented from doing what they want to do, whether that frustration comes from an adult saying, "No!" or from a physical inability to achieve what they want. It has to do with finding yourself helpless against an immovable object, and sometimes we want to bang our head against the wall; to act out our feelings.

So, we can see why we're feeling frustrated today when there are so many things we are prevented from doing, things that would make us feel better about our lives, better able to face the worries laid upon us by the current crisis. We polite folk try not to throw a tantrum, instead we scream inside, but it's not a bad idea to find some safe outlet instead: I used to find that smashing a piece of china (an unwanted one) on the floor was very satisfying. Another possibility is to try a diversionary tactic – if we can't do that, we can do this. And it is worth finding something, because otherwise the frustration can burst out in words or actions we regret. Let's take a look at Moses, Numbers 20: 1-13, the account of water from the rock. We're more used to reading the account in Exodus (Exodus 17: 1-7) but the account as told in Numbers adds an interesting insight.

The scenario is the same: in the Sinai the people are thirsty and start yet again to moan and long to return to Egypt, remembering it only as a golden time when everything was good (it wasn't!). God, given the problem, tells Moses to take his staff and, the company gathered around him, to command the rock to give up water. The people are assembled, but by now Moses is so frustrated with their moaning and complaining that he temporarily loses his cool. "Listen, you rebels. Must we get water for you out of this rock?" Then he doesn't merely speak to the rock as he was told to do, he hits it with the staff and water flows out. Do you see where his frustration has led him? Into a dramatization that suggests his actions are bringing about the miracle and worse, "Must we get water for you out of this rock." We, not God. God was not impressed that Moses had not upheld his holiness – I guess essentially putting himself on an equal footing with God - and as a result, Moses learns that he will not lead the people into the promised land.

Frustration, not dealt with, can lead any of us to actions and comments that we profoundly regret and that can affect our future. Yes, today there are many things we can't do, many things that are distressing us, so there's a need to seek God's guidance through his Spirit as to what we can do; firstly what will build us up and then how we can respond realistically and calmly to the current situation and how we can share the love of God with the people around us.

Remember, God responded immediately to bring water to the thirsty: it was Moses who turned it into something of a circus. God is still happy to bring quietly what we need, and particularly at this time to bring what we need psychologically and spiritually to cope here and now.

And bear in mind – what we remember from before this Lockdown time wasn't all good, it had its problems and annoyances too.

The rock in the Sinai from which water is reputed to have come – in the Koran, it states that Moses struck the rock twelve times, for each of the Tribes of Israel. The rock has twelve slits from which something at some time has flowed. You choose what you think!

A prayer:

We pause before God, perhaps tired, for being frustrated or angry saps our energy.

Loving God our Father, from whom streams of living water flow to cleanse us of sin, of weariness; we pray that healing flow for the world today. For many are hungry, thirsty; many live in streets littered in refuse, running with sewage; many drown in a flood of fear, deafened by sounds of fighting; many sit alone, lost, wondering how they can cope. There are people close to us who are struggling against a tide of misfortune. This grieves us and we know that it grieves you. For these situations, and so many more, we pray your healing, your peace to fill and refresh.

We pray your healing stream of living water to pour within the corridors of power, both in our own and other nations.

Bring, we pray, the stream of the Spirit's wisdom and peace where there are negotiations and hard decisions to be made, and bring the calm of that same Spirit where there is the pull of competing issues and needs.

Help all, we pray, to act from calm and not from frustration. Calmly, Lord, we look out at the world and ask that you show us the good around us today.

What good thing can we do to take our minds off things or to improve things for someone else? Show us, enable us, we ask. Help us know how to pray.

Our prayers we offer in the name of Jesus your Son our Saviour, who offers always true life in all its fullness.

Amen

St Luke

St Luke is the Patron Saint of Surgeons, physicians and artists and his special day is 18th October, the day when his life and work have been celebrated in the Church through the ages. His symbol is the ox and St Luke, author of the third Gospel and of the Acts of the Apostles, is taken to be a doctor: in Colossians 4:14 we read, "Luke, the beloved physician, and Demas greet you." He accompanied St Paul on some of his missionary journeys as in several places he writes, "we" as in Acts 16:11, "We set sail from Troas," including himself in the account.

It seems particularly appropriate to think of Luke the doctor at this time when the Lockdown is increasing, as are concerns for the NHS, but I think we also need to remember that Luke was also a man who had a particular awareness of the poor and the marginalised, the outcast. Only in his Gospel do we have the Parables of the Prodigal Son, (Luke 15:11-32) and of the Good Samaritan, (10:25-37) the outsider who did the will of God, caring for the stranger. Luke also includes several stories of women, and his account of the Nativity involves those outsiders, the shepherds. So that's a second reason to be thinking about St Luke this Sunday, at this time when the divisions in society are broadening instead of lessening.

Luke seems to have been unafraid to challenge the status quo; to show that the behaviour that the world admires is not necessarily impressing God, the parable of the Pharisee and the Tax Collector (18:9-14) being a good example of the comparisons he makes. Such stories make us pause, too – where do we stand? Do our lives, our use of money and the status we have as consumers and as literate beings reflect God's values or those of society? Do our prayers reflect God's values of justice and peace for all the earth? Interesting and uncomfortable questions that are worth asking ourselves.

What we can probably agree on is that the world is desperately in need of healing. There is healing in the medical sense, the sense that's at the forefront of our minds now. There is healing needed of the rifts in society. But healing in the psychological and spiritual sense is also vital for us all at this moment. People who have contracted the COVID-19 virus find, in some cases, that there are unforeseen effects: "long COVID", as it's now known, which includes physical effects and mental ones, including a fuzziness of mind, apparently. But recovery from any serious illness brings after-effects; finding you've recovered from such as a heart attack or cancer is joyous, but many people then find it difficult to return to 'normal' life. We find that somewhere along the line, the experience has changed normality: our values have changed. This will equally apply to each of us when we eventually emerge from the abnormality of this Lockdown to find a new, full life again.

I suspect that society will need a similar healing and gentleness, and it brings us back to the values we hold – are they society's or God's? Life as a Christian is not easy, nor is the way always clear, but the need for faithfulness in prayer, in study remains a constant. And, I'd suggest, the need to rest sometimes!

Luke is also Patron Saint of Artists. He is credited with producing the first icon of the Virgin Mary, the Convent of Sydnaya in Syria having what is claimed to be one of Luke's icons. Maybe the other thing he's suggesting is to look at the world with an artist's eye and see the changes, the beauty and to offer it, and all we can make of beauty, to God.

Convent of Sydnaya

A prayer:

For a moment just bring to mind the doctors at your own GP practice, and doctors who have helped you through the years, maybe surgeons who have made a huge difference to your own, or a loved one's, life. Bring, too, those you know who are ill or in any kind of distress.

Eternal, Living God our Father, you sent your Son Jesus that, through his death and rising, all may find life in its fullness. We praise and thank you for those of faith and of none that you have called to work as doctors and surgeons, for the skills they offer, for their dedication to their calling. At this time when all doctors are having to work under unusual conditions – distancing, masked when they see patients, trying to diagnose through telephone consultations, unable to offer the reassurance of touch where there is distress, we ask a special gift of your Holy Spirit to bring understanding, and the right words to say.

We ask, Lord, strength when they are weary, and the knowledge that people do understand and sympathise with the pressures under which all NHS staff are working today. We thank you for the calling and skill of surgeons and the seemingly incredible outcomes they are often able to achieve. But we are conscious that sometimes, despite their best efforts, surgery does not succeed, and we ask your peace and healing touch in the distress felt by patients and those close to them, when the outcome is not what they wanted, and that is also felt by the surgeons and their teams.

Loving Lord, we know that sometimes death is a healing, and we bring those doctors and other medical staff who work in hospices, or with the dying in hospitals, in care homes and at home. As they help people move beyond this life to the next, may it be with calm and dignity.

Thank you, Lord, for those who, themselves unafraid, help others face the end of their life here on earth calmly and at peace, loved just as they are.

We ask this in Jesus' name.
Amen

Sharing

© Helen E Gordon

When I trained as a Primary teacher way back in the sixties, one of the things we were taught was how we should respond if asked a question to which we didn't know the answer. (If?!) Under no circumstances, we were told, should we pretend we knew or make up an answer, because at some point we'd be sure to be proved wrong, and that would do our reputations no good. Instead, we were to say, "That's a good question, let's look up the answer together."

Fine, but it didn't need a child of Mensa-level intelligence to realise that particular response was usually code for "I don't know." An alternative –

"I need to double-check that" - was a slightly face-saving way out with the same result, namely, you shared the process of discovery.

The truth, of course, is that none of we mere humans know everything, yet somehow we long for some people to be all-knowing. Parents and teachers when we are small. Leaders in many spheres of life when we are bigger.

I'm sure you can see where I'm going with this. We are living in a time of not-knowing: though knowledge of the COVID-19 virus is increasing, much is still mystery and as for knowing what works against it, what we can do to mitigate its effects . . . well. But we are also living in a time when some people share their opinions as if they knew it all when they don't, and this confuses us still further. Also, none of it is good for the health of those in leadership.

Moses, carrying the burden of leadership of the People of Israel, was exhausted, a fact his visiting father-in-law, Jethro, noticed and wisely advised that he chose Elders to share in his burden. (Exodus 18: 13-27) He did as advised, and no doubt slept more soundly.

St. Paul struggled too. The Christians in Corinth were squabbling between themselves so much, listening to this one and that one (sound familiar?), that he had to feed them a liquid-diet Gospel rather than the 'meaty' Gospel that they should have been able to take in (1 Corinthians 3: 1-3) and that was a loss to them as a community and to the people they could have helped.

So we look to Jesus who, having proved to his disciples who he was and how much they could trust in him, came to the point when they could take more truth (John 15:7-17).

"I do not call you servants any longer, because the servant does not know what the master is doing; but I have called you friends, because I have made known to you everything that I have heard from my Father." (Verse 15)

No matter how old or wise we may be, there is no-one on earth who knows it all, not only about the new virus, but also about life and about faith itself and the more we have the humility to assess what we are hearing and to share in the learning process, the better for us and, ultimately, for the world. This sounds hard, but remember, Jesus trusts us – he calls us friends, too! He's given us the Holy Spirit to help us, to help us always.

I love this picture. They're studying a Roman inscription which, in spite of considerable combined knowledge, proved indecipherable – we don't always get an answer to our questions! What we needed, of course was a bona fide Roman to explain it.

A prayer:

Living Lord, thank you for your gift to us of intellect and of insight to use for the good of all, and for curiosity, for the searching mind that will not give up until an issue is fully explored, and conclusions reached even if that conclusion is to admit to a not knowing.

Thank you, too, that intellect and insight come in many forms to create the right balance needed in life. May we be ever willing to listen to the least as well as to the mighty. In these times when questions seem to pile hard upon one another, when definite answers are sought although they cannot be given, we pray that leaders within all areas of life may have the humility to pause, to listen, to admit the fractional nature of their knowledge, to trust in the ordinary person's capacity to understand, to consider, to hope and pray.

In a world of 'influencers' who shape so much thinking, we pray the wisdom of the Spirit that those of influence, whether in politics, the media or in matters of faith, may pause, talk over with trusted friends what they are thinking, really reflect upon the power they have gained and seek to use it wisely for the benefit of all people and even of the earth itself.

Lord, with the world, we admit that we want certainty even when we know that's not possible. We seek leaders who know everything, even when we know that's not reasonable. We are afraid. We are lost. Lord, hold us in our fear and our lostness.

By your Spirit, guide us all into peace. We are afraid and lost, but we are also followers of Jesus who faced the powers of darkness, of fear and of ignorance and prejudice, and who trusts us to do likewise. We pray for ourselves, when others may be looking to us to see how we react.

May we be strong in how we deal with the present moment, but also humble in admitting, but not dwelling upon, our own sorrows.

Loving Lord God our Father, who is in perfect unity with the Son and the Spirit, draw us into a true unity of heart and mind, that we may face whatever the world has to give with a true peace and a shared wisdom.

We ask it in Jesus' name.
Amen

All Saints and All Souls

A ll Saints Day, the day we remember the saints as a group rather than individuals, is 1st November, thus giving us Hallowe'en, a shortened form of 'All Hallows' Eve'. The difficulty for the church was that remembering the saints was less exciting than imagining the ghoulies and ghosties and four-legged beasties against which an ancient prayer guarded you, and to divert attention from the night of 31st October, All Souls Day was instituted for 2nd November as the day for remembering those who have died. Some cultures have their own 'day of the dead,' at which they seem to have a very jolly time, but the quiet All Souls has never really caught on in this country, outside of the church, most preferring to be frightened witless on 31st October instead.

I wonder whether we hold on to Hallowe'en because of a reluctance to think about real death? Look at the way we rarely hear people say someone has died; they have "passed" and not even "passed away." Passed what, I facetiously want to ask. Passed Go and failed to collect £200 pounds? Of course, I keep such thoughts to myself. Until now, that is!

But the Pandemic has forced us to remember that our lives are finite, and the recent upturn in cases earlier in the year than expected, along with new regulations, has unsettled us profoundly.

But the truth is that we are finite, and so what we do with our lives matters. Can we be saintly? Probably we'd all want to say, "No way!" but the early Christians are described as saints (eg. Ephesians 1:1, Acts 9: 32 in most translations), so maybe we should be less hard upon ourselves. We are not required to float in a cloud of holiness but to live our saintly lives in the messy everyday.

I think of a member of one of my first churches. By the time I met her, she had no short-term memory whatsoever, but had an open, welcoming attitude to everyone. She had lived in the same house for many, many years and was well known; the children, she told me, would come to her window and do a little dance for her. I worried a bit whether they were actually mocking her, but it turned out that I was way off the mark. Speaking after her funeral to one of the many neighbours who'd come along, I was told that as children they'd always gone to her rather than to their parents when they fell down or were unhappy and, she said, it had been lovely when their own children had done exactly the same, going to 'Aunty Eva' rather than mum for a sticking plaster. And from her I found that, indeed, they had done little dances in front of her window to make her laugh. Now, I knew from the Church Secretary that things hadn't been good for her in her life, but she smiled and loved always and said nothing of the negative things. I think she would be surprised at the joyful reception she received in Heaven. A latterly-absent-minded saint.

Or what about these four 'saints' of Nonconformity pictured in stained glass in Jesmond URC? Men who would never have called themselves saints, but whose lives and work had a huge impact.

Our imperfect selves are the selves God loves. No amount of assumed piety impresses God (Luke 18:9-14).

A saint can be someone who reflects the light God brings to a dark time.

A saint could be you!

A desire to love God more; a real desire to see his kingdom come in our world and a willingness to try to help the kingdom come in our own little corner of the world by our own quiet prayers and small good deeds, especially in times when people are feeling lost and in the dark – surely persisting in this way of living is the way of true saintliness.

Norway 2014

It seems to me that this picture illustrates our calling as saints – the light God shines upon us always is there to be reflected so that others can see and find their own joy. The light breaks through the dark clouds if we are around to see and share it.

Pause for a moment and think of the people you know who have been saintly in their giving of themselves; the people who seem to brighten up the day just by being there and being themselves. Thank God for them.

A prayer:

Loving God, with whom is light and joy everlasting, thank you for those people who have reflected your light in times when it has seemed very dark, those who, just by being themselves, have brought light wherever they were. Thank you that such people are still around us, often living difficult lives themselves in places and situations where darkness seems to prevail.

We pray for saints who live on run-down housing estates, in refugee camps, in sweat shops, in prisons, in places we know or have heard about, places that make us shudder; those saints who absorb your peace and give it away freely, and sometimes at their own cost. When they feel low and weary, may they know that others think of them and pray for them and may they know that, as you walked the way before them in the life, ministry and death of Jesus, you understand them and love them to the uttermost.

Lord, saintliness seems a concept far from us. We do not feel saintly, especially when the little irritations and the big problems of life wear us down. Help us remember that you understand us, too, and the difficulties we face in life, and that you will never take from us the wisdom of your Spirit and the love of Jesus.

Give us, we pray, the strength and purpose to be your true saints, wherever we are.

We ask it in Jesus' name.
Amen

Here we go again!

© Helen E Gordon

As I heard the announcement that Lockdown was back, the above title came straight to mind. But later, as the words went through my head, other words imposed themselves: the chorus of the song, Jolly Good Company:

> Here we are again
> happy as can be,
> all good pals and jolly good company.
>
> Raymond Wallace 1931

I'm pretty sure this was one of the songs sung by the music hall group, the Novocastrians, of which my paternal grandfather was part, ordinary working people who rehearsed and performed in their scant spare time, taking their show around Newcastle Working Men's Clubs. My grandfather accompanied the singing on piano and was one half of a comedy duo: he, dressed suavely complete with top hat and with silver-topped cane and his 'stooge' shabbily dressed – my grandmother prized a photograph of them in costume. Though all this ended by my early childhood, I can remember he and my father occasionally breaking into songs from the repertoire.

This one is an interesting little song, written during a time of hardship, sardonic in tone and quite relevant today even when few actually feel like singing, were it allowed, as we enter a second Lockdown.

As ever, we have a choice. We either turn in on ourselves, moan and make ourselves and others miserable, or we make the most of what we can do.

But, you may say, what about our 'jolly good pals', those dear to us we will be prevented from meeting? We still have many means of communicating with others, far more than people had when this song was written, or than when families were separated in World Wars One and Two depending only on scarce cards or letters. Even if we don't do Zoom or Skype and all the rest, we can phone family and friends for a chat. We could even – radical thought! – write a letter! Nothing to say? Come on – we can always think of something, a funny story, something we've noticed as we've looked out or gone for a walk. Trivia can be the beginning of a good conversation.

Communication matters because to cope, we need each other, just as the Music Hall group needed the whole of the cast – and needed to be willing to expend time and energy to bring some light to others. "Bear one another's burdens, and in this way you will fulfil the law of Christ." said St. Paul (Galatians 6:2) as he urged the Galatians to keep going in faith. A verse worth learning and pondering.

Bearing one another's burdens doesn't mean stripping the supermarket shelves of things we 'might' need. It means looking out for the other, waving a greeting, smiling if you're outside and maskless, keeping others in your thoughts and above all, praying hard, for others and for the world. And, however we can, being jolly good company!

Also in Galatians – Galatians 5:22-26 – is Paul's admonition to live guided by the Holy Spirit, whose fruit is "love, joy, peace, patience, kindness, generosity, faithfulness, gentleness and self-control." (Galatians 5:22) It seems to me that these are qualities massively needed at this moment, perhaps now more than ever.

A prayer:

Eternal God our Father, you are love and life. In your Son Jesus you have shown us how to live a love-motivated life, responsive to the needs of others while we also take care of ourselves.

Knowing that you call upon us to pray for and help your kingdom of peace and justice to come, we bring our concerns for the world.

We bring those who live lives starved of love: children who are neglected, adults trapped into loveless relationships, all who are abused, often in the false name of 'caring.'

We bring those who find life joyless, often driving others from them by their own attitude, and those for whom life is joyless because it is so unremittingly harsh.

We pray a gentle light, a tender laughter, your healing love, a surprise of joy.

We bring the earth, in need of peace. Peace from terror, war and struggle. From Lockdown. Peace for creation itself, over-used, exhausted. As we approach Remembrance Sunday, we are even more aware of the cost of war and, though we cannot see how it can come to be, earnestly we pray for true peace.

We bring with thanksgiving the quality that is kindness. The big acts of kindness that surprise us and the ordinary kindnesses offered freely to one another. Help us, Lord, to be kind.

We bring with thanksgiving those who demonstrate goodness, generosity of heart. Those who, having little, yet give much. Those who have been blessed with much and share what they have. We pray, at this troubled time, a generosity of heart for all.

We bring with thanksgiving those who encourage us by their faithfulness in you, and we bring those who have lost faith – in people, in you, Lord. Touch them, we pray, with the gentle presence of your Spirit.

We bring the need of the world for gentleness, gentleness of thought, word, of action, gentleness towards self and to one another.

We bring our need of self-control. Help all people, Lord, the powerful and the powerless, to pause, to seek the guidance of your Spirit, that we might be enabled to show the way of Jesus to our hurting world, for it is in his name we offer this prayer.

Amen

The Way Ahead

You are driving cheerily along and are faced with the first, then (if we miss it) the second sign. Once I only discovered the road was closed when I found workmen digging it up in front of me – "There's a sign back there telling you," said one of the men and I was asking myself how I'd missed it when I glanced in the rear-view mirror and saw a queue of at least six cars behind me. The warning notice had blown down.

We may well feel that we came to Lockdown Mark 2 with barely any warning. The way ahead of us closed quickly and we can't go where we wanted. We can't visit who we want to. Church services are suspended again. So, how have you responded?

If we're driving, we can keep going, knock over the sign and perhaps drive straight into a large hole in the ground – and get ourselves arrested. In Lockdown, we can ignore all the rules and advice and end up infected - and perhaps arrested. A choice, but an unwise one!

If we're driving, we can entrust ourselves to a Sat Nav which may lead us along new roads; perhaps the Lockdown equivalent is using Zoom or Skype, or live-streaming. Or we might choose to work out our own route, which may or may not be more efficient, but which may suit us better or surprise us, leading us through new scenery. It might slow us down when that's exactly what we need.

Or we can just give up and turn back home and be miserable. Well, it's a choice, but withdrawing and focusing on what we can't rather than can do isn't a good option, personally or collectively.

In Acts 16:6-10, we have Paul facing a 'no through road' when he was "forbidden by the Holy Spirit to speak the word in Asia" and then found his attempt to go into Bithynia prevented by "the Spirit of Jesus." There's been a lot of thought and ink expended on what this means, but for the present purpose it reminds us that having restrictions placed upon you can actually lead into new areas: having been baulked of doing what he planned, Paul had a vision in a dream of a man from Macedonia asking him to come there to speak to them, and so the journey took a new turn. In his letter to the Roman Christians, Paul speaks of his longing to see them, for their mutual benefit (Romans 1:8-12), but he was to reach them and testify to them only as a prisoner.

I'm thinking of all this because I was saddened on Remembrance Sunday to see how many organisations and churches took the view that, because what we've always done in the past isn't possible, then we do nothing. Having been involved in a short outdoor socially distanced, masked and tracked-and-traced, remembrance ceremony (no names, but you know who you are!), I've seen that such a time can bring people together and be profoundly moving, though being woken by 'The Last Post' on bugles probably wasn't on the wish-list of those having a long lie-in.

This Lockdown came upon us quickly with little time to plan, but now we have some thinking space and I believe that surely the times in which we're living are, of all times, when we need to think outside the box. Within the regulations, and keeping safety always high in our thinking, we can still find ways to work together, to build one another up and to share our faith.

Maybe everything is confusing for you at the moment.

First of all, pause and take a breath. Look for a new route. We're not really alone on the journey!

We can think of each other, pray for each other, smile at each other. And laugh!

A prayer:

Loving, Living God our Father, thank you for the opportunities you offer us day by day to live our lives prayerfully and meaningfully, and thank you for our minds, our creative selves, that can devise new ways forward, new ways of sharing the Good News of Christ.

We praise and bless you that it is that creativity that streams from you, a creativity that first brought all things into being in rich and wonderful variety, a creativity that your Spirit brings to each one in rich and wonderfully different ways.

This brings joy, Lord, but we are aware that many people are feeling very low, this second Lockdown bringing a specific sadness and anxiety. We think of those who, living alone, can see only their own sense of loneliness and who, by their negativity, push away the very people who would normally talk with them. We think of those worried about their livelihood: those who fear probable redundancy, those who have small shops, who run small organisations, and those worried how they can continue to offer social care and support to the needy.

We bring those working within the world of medicine, with the present stresses they face. May they all know that they are not alone, that others think of them, pray for them and, if needed, will speak up for them.

We think of governments of the world, faced with the Lockdown and its economic fallout.

For all, Lord, we earnestly seek the wisdom of the Holy Spirit to guide and eyes and ears open to the truth.

We think of the United States of America following this election of a new President, and pray for a good transition and a growing calm to heal divisions. May your Spirit guide and restore; bring peace and joy.

In this season of remembrance, we think of the wars of past years and mourn that war continues in so many parts of the world; that terror still seizes many; that unjust regimes flourish. Earnestly we pray the peace that Christ brings, the peace the world alone cannot give.

We think of the Church, asking the guidance of your Spirit that we may faithfully share the Gospel of Christ, not only among ourselves, but with the communities around us, aware of the great anxiety that is gripping so many.

We seek your blessing, Lord, upon the work, the words and the acts of kindness.

This prayer we offer in Jesus' name.
Amen

Down from a pedestal!

It's a long way to the ground!

At the present time, we seem to be hearing a lot about loss of political power so it's worth thinking about how people cope with a fall from power – or how people try to deny that they've lost, of course! It must be hard, when you have had a position of power and authority to have to come back down to earth; for any of us to be praised and held up as someone special is a good feeling, and the temptation to hold onto that feeling must be strong.

I guess that at a very basic level, survival depends upon having something of a competitive streak – survival of the fittest and all that - but this is normally tempered by a concern for our companions. Things go wrong when we are persuaded that we have some right to the highest positions, to the best of this and that, when we are persuaded that we have gifts that in reality we have only in small measure. We like to succeed, and the idea of winning is all around us: if you think not, just check your television programme listings and count how many competitions you find there! And then we have the fact that today's society lauds the powerful and the people who make most noise, those who constantly put themselves forward.

All this is not new and, sadly, is a feature of faith too. In many parts of the Old Testament, we find the concept that wealth is a sign of God's blessing, something that has been adopted by the so-called 'Prosperity Gospel' churches, where one is expected to pray for wealth and possessions, to expect these to come to you as a kind of reward for your faith.

I cannot reconcile this with what was the radical teaching of Jesus, that wealth is not a sign of holiness. To shocked disciples, he said that it was easier for a camel to go through the eye of a needle than for a rich man to make it to heaven (Matthew 19:21-26). No doubt to similarly surprised hearers, he commended the small offering of the widow as being of more significance than the ostentatious giving of the rich (Mark 12:41-44). And as far as worldly power was concerned, Jesus faced it quietly, courageously and ultimately prevailed.

We really need to keep this before us at the present time. It is the Kingdom of God which we seek and work to bring, a kingdom of justice and of peace, of quietness and not ostentation. I'm aware that this means we will be rowing against the tide, but so be it.

On a simple level, we maybe need to try to encourage a thinking that doesn't put people on pedestals or that teaches that we shouldn't have to fail. Yes, we strive to be the best we can be, but the best we can be will not be perfection! It's interesting that I've heard a number of people saying that children are now needing to be taught how to cope with failure and, as an ex-teacher, I agree. Failing in a particular task does not mean that you're a failure as a person! Learning to fail and learning from that failure is a step towards real maturity of soul.

To close, a lovely statement of Jesus' for everyone who feels small, or even who's fallen off a pedestal:

"But many who are first will be last, and the last will be first."
(Mark 10:31)

The ruined Church of St Simeon Stylites, in Syria. He was a holy man who lived on top of a column by the main road, people coming to him for advice and, I suspect, to gawp. The lump of stone on the pillar base in the centre of the picture is all that's left of his column after centuries of souvenir-seekers had carved out pieces. I confess that though I admire the Desert Fathers and Mothers, who hid away in remote spots but welcomed anyone who came to them for help, I do not admire the stylites who strike me as publicity seekers. And this is all that's left.

It's good just to be the people we are wherever we are.

Think of those who have great authority or popularity. They need our prayers.

A prayer:

There was a hymn popular in the seventies, "If I were a butterfly", that said, "But I just thank you Father, for making me, me." That's not an easy line for many of us to sing and to really believe.

Loving God and Father of all, Creator and sustainer of all, thank you that we each have our own gifts to use for the good of all. Thank you for those who have great and obvious gifts of artistry, of management, of invention, so many gifts, so many people.

But we thank you, too, for those who have gifts of encouragement, the people who make us feel good just by being there and being themselves, those who would deny that they have anything great to offer, and yet who give themselves unsparingly for the building up of others. Lord, we cannot do without such people: help us show them our love.

We pray for those who have gifts that are enabling the development of a COVID-19 vaccine and for those offering themselves to test it out, aware that many are within the Health Service and already giving so much.

We pray for all doctors, nurses, carers and all within our hospitals, clinics, surgeries and care homes, that by your Spirit they may be given strength when they are weary.

Give, we pray, we ordinary folk the insight to note when people are stressed by their work, by their worries. May we be a quiet presence to be with them and support them.

Lord, when we are tempted to put people on a pedestal, help us pause; when we are tempted by even a tiny pedestal for ourselves, help us pause and remember the words of Jesus that many who are first will be last, and the last will be first.

Thank you that Jesus chose a quiet way that led to new life, full life for us all, and that we are called to follow that way of service to you and for the good of all creation.

We pray in Jesus' name.
Amen

Advent Sunday

Traditionally, many churches have an Advent wreath, one candle being lit each Sunday in Advent until all four are lit on the Sunday prior to Christmas. On Christmas Eve or Christmas morning, a central white candle is lit, the whole symbolising not so much the count-down to Christmas as a reminder of the coming of the Light of the World, Jesus.

I don't know if you've ever waited to watch a sunrise. If my memory serves me right (and increasingly it doesn't!) the only time I've done this was in 1993, when, as part of a group of pilgrims to the Holy Land first spending two nights in the Sinai, I watched the sunrise from Mount Sinai – not from the top, as by the time we had climbed to the open space where the camels and their Bedouin drivers rested, my knee was protesting mightily. Here a few of us waited as the camel drivers lay on the ground, wrapped themselves in their thick cloaks and dozed, just as their ancestors had done for thousands of years, while the camels sat, chewing meditatively and staring into space, as camels have done for thousands of years.

There were intimations of the coming dawn: the blue-black sky over the distant horizon began to develop shades of grey, revealing the mountain range beyond and then gradually the light intensified from behind those distant peaks until, after a surprisingly long while, the tip of the sun could be sighted. At that point, it became light very quickly; the Bedouin woke and started to load up the slightly reluctant camels and our fellow pilgrims began to appear from the higher reaches of the mountain.

That experience tells me that we're on the right lines with our Advent candles, showing that the true light comes, not as a great lightning-flash, but after a gradual preparation.

One of the psalms I love is Psalm 130, with its image of waiting for God being like a watchman waiting for the dawn: we sense the intensity of the sentry standing on the city walls longing for the light to come so that any attack will be shown up rather than sensed amid the shadows. There's an image there for us too, at this time when we are aware of a COVID-19 'attacker' out there and, like the sentry on night-watch, lonely, weary of it all and longing for the light to come.

I suspect that what we want is a sudden turn-around: the almost frantic enthusiasm with which the news of vaccines is being seized upon shows us how much we want everything to be light and hope immediately. The truth, I fear, is that like the dawn, our release from the shadows in which we currently live will be very gradual; we will see forward only bit by bit. It may be that, like the sentry, we will have to hold out a bit longer, even though we are lonely and tired.

Or maybe we can take a leaf out of the Bedouins' and camels' books, and rest while we can and look about us while we can. Many people said that the initial Lockdown had given them time to notice the detail of creation in a way they'd been too busy to do before, and we can still do that even in autumn/winter. We also have time to think – I suspect that part of the reason these thoughts and prayer have caught on to the extent they have has something to do with the fact we are actually giving ourselves time to reflect. So, we keep going: Christ, who brings an inextinguishable light to the world is come, and is coming.

So, if you feel like it, curl up in your cloak-equivalent and have a little sleep. Or think, reflect on what you see and hear. And watch . . . Jesus comes through the chaos and shadow quietly, gently, step by quiet step, bringing light and peace to the earth. Come, Lord Jesus!

Worth considering – at what stage in the dawn would you put the Lockdown now? Or where would you put society today: in the shadowy early stages of dawn or in a state of increasing light?

A prayer:

Living God our Father, we rejoice in the light that Jesus brings, a
light that penetrates the darkness of sin, of fear, to bring
forgiveness and hope of a new dawn. The dawn of a new day, the
light radiating across the sky in a multitude of shades brings with
it its own peace, its own hope of new beginning.

By your Spirit, Lord, guide us in seeing and following the light
that leads us along right paths into your kingdom of justice and
of peace. At this time of year when so many thoughts are turned
towards celebrations of Christmas: a meeting together of
people, a sharing of gifts, a time of feasting, we pray for the calm
guiding of your Holy Spirit in the changed circumstances of this
year.

We bring those who are anxious at the thought they will not be
able to meet together in the numbers they are accustomed to
doing, those with a fear of being alone, those who are anxious
about the spending because they have little money or because
the future of their employment is precarious.

For all we ask a calm, an understanding that the love shared
among families and friends lives on, whether we are together or
apart, whether we are rich or poor.

At this time of uncertainty, we bring those who have important
decisions to make, longing that the powerful might hear the cry
of the powerless and that all may work towards that day when
nations look beyond their own boundaries to see fellow human
beings and not enemies.

In a disturbed world, Lord, we pray peace, especially in those
places currently locked into conflict and where the innocent
suffer, and the earth is despoiled.

At this time of shortening days, we rejoice in the special quality of the light, in the glorious colours of sunrise and sunset. Conscious that many people feel low in the darker months, we pray a special light and joy to fill all our hearts and minds, a light that glows within and shines forth to share your peace with all we meet, just through your love shining from our lives.

Thank you, Lord, for each and every day, blessed by the light of Jesus, in whose name we pray.

Amen

Is it worth it?

© Helen E Gordon

We have heard a great deal about Christmas recently, and many people are relieved to be able to see family over the holiday season, but also confused as to who they can see and how many there should be and . . . and . . . so many questions.

If my walk yesterday was anything to go by, it has all focused people's minds wonderfully: I found people more courteous in stepping aside. Perhaps, I wonder, has Christmas become the carrot that is persuading people to take the virus seriously and to follow the guidelines? The other question is one we each need to resolve as best we see fit: is meeting up at

Christmas worth the risk of spreading the virus? It makes the normally knotty decision of whether to go to the in-laws this Christmas seem the simplest of choices.

Then there is the on-going talk of people wearing pyjamas all day and even of letting personal hygiene slip (badly!), all because they're not going to work and no-one will see them, so it's not worth bothering. Well, if your friends are starting to shuffle aside to stand up-wind of you, then you certainly have a problem, but for the rest of us, let me tell you of cries that I've heard so, so often.

"When you live alone, it's not worth cooking just for yourself." "Oh, I don't bother putting up Christmas decorations, there's only me." If I respond with the fact that I live alone and do both of those things, I am told that it's alright for me, I'm used to being alone. Given that I have lived alone for the majority of my life, there is a little truth there, but let's just think for a moment.

Much of what we all do is, quite rightly, for the sake of others but how should we behave towards ourselves? In the Book of Genesis we read that God created Adam in his own image (Genesis 1:26a). You don't have to be a Creationist to realise there's a hint there that God thinks something of us, individually. Then again, we cheerfully declare that Christ died for us – that in his love, God sent his only Son so that everyone who believes in him may not perish but may have eternal life (John 3:16). A study of the Bible focusing on the passages that tell of God's love would turn up even more evidence and begs the question, if God loves us so much, should we not respond with a bit of self-care? Not with self-obsession, just a bit of self care.

A verse has stuck with me this week: when Jesus spoke against ostentatious fasting, making yourself look as miserable as you feel (Matthew 6: 16-18), he said, "put oil on your head and wash your face, so that your fasting may be seen not by others but by your Father who is in secret." It's a good reminder that our relationship with God is of massive importance and that he knows and understands us in all our ups and downs. Yes, we feel confused and conflicted just now and I know myself that it's very hard when we're alone to motivate ourselves, all too easy to think, "Oh, it's not worth bothering," and to make it clear by our behaviour that's what we think. Then the dullness of the weather and the way that the Lockdown seems to go on and on mitigates against grasping the moment, but maybe this is the very time we need to hold onto the fact that we are loved of God and it's worth bothering for him – and for the sake of the few people we do see!

After all, he bothered for us!

A prayer:

Lord God our Father, thank you that you love us with a love so great we can barely imagine it, a love that longs for us to have full lives within a creation that is as much at ease with us as we with it, a love that longs to offer forgiveness and new life even when we hide away, fearful at what we are and what we do, fearful at our failures.

We come today conscious that there are many people feeling very low, thinking "Why bother?" about so many aspects of their lives, many feeling a general frustration and anger. Loving Father, may the light Jesus brings touch each life with hope and a nascent joy.

We bring those who need the constant acclamation of others in order to believe in themselves, and in order to find purpose in life, especially those who are feeling lost and alone at this time. Loving Father, may the light Jesus brings shine within their lives to show the value of who they are and what they do.

We bring those whose mental health is much affected by the continuing Lockdown, and those who work within straightened circumstances to bring support and healing, and those who, though affected themselves by their own fragile health, yet bring understanding, hope and joy to others. Loving Father, may your Holy Spirit give them perseverance and strength and the knowledge that others remember and pray for them.

We bring those working in areas of the world where many are dispossessed of home and family, where people are holding desperately onto a sense of who they are and longing for security. Loving Father, may your Holy Spirit bring wisdom to all people of influence that they may seek justice and peace for the whole world.

In the coming weeks we all have decisions to make at a time when it is so hard to find the energy to do so, when our minds feel like jelly and the future uncertain. Remind us, Lord, that here we are within the season of Advent, looking to the coming of Jesus, sign of your love for the world and bringer of light and hope. Help us raise eyes and hearts to him, that our hearts might be filled with his love and his light, now and in all the days to come.

We ask it in Jesus' name.
Amen

Christmas Cards

T is the season of Christmas cards, and the image above is of the first such. The year was 1843 and Henry Cole, a busy man, was faced with a vast number of Christmas letters (the new postal service had encouraged a real spate of letter-writing) and courtesy dictated that you should answer each one. Thus he asked an artist friend, J.C. Horsley, to design this triptych – a family enjoying a Christmas meal, flanked by images of people helping the poor - and had a thousand copies printed on card by a London printer. There was space at the top for the recipient's name, and so began the Christmas Card. I doubt he had any idea what he'd started.

We still use the Christmas card to contact people who are on the edge of our friendship circles, but it can become something of a burden unless you like writing out dozens of cards. Also, many folk now question the morality of destroying so many trees in the process.

The image of the first card is interesting and really deserves a reflection all to itself, but suffice it for the moment to look at this as his own personal image of Christmas; you might like to see how it compares with your own. Strangely, Charles Dickens' A Christmas Carol was published in the same year, with its combination of celebration along with care for the poor.

Today, we have a vast array of images to choose from, but what I've always found interesting is that once I started to train for ministry, I stopped receiving any humorous cards at all. It was the same when I was in hospital a long while ago for surgery: my Get Well cards were terribly serious to the point that one could easily have doubled as an 'In Sympathy' card. Bit premature, I thought.

But Valentine's Day fell while I was there and a nurse dumped a pile of cards on my bed saying, "There's got to be a Valentine among that lot!" And there was, as I shouted out loud in surprise. My fellow patients perked up. One decided that in honour of the day, she'd do her hair properly for her husband visiting, and another patient, who was an ex-hairdresser, did it for her. And then did another patient's hair! The person who sent me the Valentine to cheer me up (I've no idea who it was) could never have imagined the positive effect that card would have on people whose self-image had been badly dented through surgery.

Surely the point of sending cards is to share our love, our concern, and to lift the spirits of the other, because knowing that you're remembered and valued is so important. I'm going to end with that great letter-writer, St. Paul, and the close of the second letter to Timothy (2 Timothy 4: 9-22). Here he is desperately lonely, deserted by many and hanging on to his faith in the power of God to hold him, yet still sending greetings to those he was remembering fondly and passing on greetings from others. I guess being the conduit of love and concern helped him in his own loneliness, as it can do for us in our troubled times.

Keeping in contact in a meaningful way matters, however we choose to do it. Some cards, both traditional and e-cards are beautiful artworks in themselves and can stir in us a sense of wonder, and today so much can be shared via the internet if you choose not to write an actual letter.

It's perhaps especially important this year, when our physical meeting up has been curtailed or even prevented, to keep loving contact with those nearby and those who are on our minds, but physically distant from us, to show that we hold them always in our hearts and prayers.

A prayer:

Loving God, Father of all, at this season when all seems so different, when all our usual approach to Christmas seems to have been changed we come to you in thanksgiving for your amazing gift to us of your Son, Jesus, setting aside all glory to be born within human constraints, in humility.

This sign of new life offered from your own love is one we feel we cannot deserve, and yet it is offered freely. Lord, your love is beyond our comprehension. Remembering that gift, we also remember the many people for whom the giving of gifts brings immense pressure through lack of money or unrealistic expectations. As we recall the simplicity of your birth, Lord Jesus, we long for an acceptance of the realities of our own lives, of who we are, and what we might achieve in your strength.

At this difficult time, we pray a special gift of the Holy Spirit to guide those who have important decisions to make, that they may be motivated by a desire to enhance the life of the world, and not to seek to grab the biggest share, the most glory.

In a world in turmoil, we pray your peace.
In a sick world, we pray your healing.
In a weary world, we pray your strength.

Already cards are arriving, some bringing great joy, others bringing sorrow as we hear of the losses and problems of our friends far away. Give us, we pray, the right words to speak or write that will bring comfort and hope, or that will increase the joy of the sender. Help us too, when we have sad news to share, to have the right words to speak or write so that others may understand our own sorrow but not be overwhelmed by it.

We bring those whose needs – social, physical or psychological – lie much upon our own hearts. We pray healing; we pray peace. At this busy time, we thank you for those artists who design cards to appear in shops and on the internet.

Thank you for the often Spirit-inspired beauty, and for the way in which we can be drawn into the scene and find there a peace beyond all we had hoped.

May that peace, the peace that Jesus brings, fill the earth this day and always. We ask it in Jesus' name.

Amen

Christ comes silently

Luke 2: 1-7

O n Saturday 12th, I joined the Supporters' Day of the Bumblebee Conservation Trust – on Zoom, and excellent it was. Those who know me well are aware that I am passionate, not to say obsessive, about bumblebees, and when we can meet up again, I'm happy to come and speak about them at your church or organisation, but what possible connection can they have with Christmas? Just in my mind! I shall explain.

Honeybees, as you know, all hibernate for winter. Bumblebees – our wild furry bees – are different. In late summer, the new queens emerge, mate and go into hibernation while the rest of the nest dies. The new queens, carrying the potential life of a whole colony, find a warm place, usually underground, compost heaps being one such place, and sleep away autumn and winter, emerging in early spring when they have to find a good nesting place that already has some 'bedding' for warmth – under your shed or in an abandoned mouse's nest, for example – where they begin to lay eggs in a little wax pot they have created, sitting on this as birds do to keep it warm (the nest has to be 30°C), flying out to feed quickly then returning to the nest. This is repeated until enough adults emerge to be nursemaids and foragers, and she can focus on full-time egg-laying.

One single bee, working quite alone and carrying massive responsibility, begins a chain reaction of life, not only for her own colony, but, though the pollinating the bees do, of life for plants, animals, us - life for the whole planet. She is vulnerable. She needs all the help we can give her.

This made me think of the Nativity of Jesus. One single child, vulnerable to all the dangers around him, needing the protection of parents, one child who carried within him life for us all. Logically and sensibly, it doesn't sound like a good way to begin a movement that was going to change the world, but God does not always behave in the way we expect nor when we expect it; God takes risks and to mitigate these, needs us to play our part.

In Jesus' life, Mary and Joseph did that initial protecting, cherishing and learning, then the disciples took on the learning task so that they could go out further, and the message of new life be extended to the world. As I thought of the small bee, instinctively throwing her whole life into ensuring a future, I was really brought up sharp as I thought about Jesus, who had a conscious understanding of all that he was personally risking, throwing his whole life into ensuring a future that was about real, true life in its fulness. And the risk was enormous.

It's very easy to get caught up into the trappings of Christmas and lose sight of what is essential, but maybe this year, when we're not able to hurry about catching up with people or rushing from one carol service to another, we might have more time to contemplate the significance of the quiet, individual part we are all called upon to play. Maybe we all need to learn that the coming of Christ is not about a big, social event, is not entirely about what we do together, but is also a quiet, solitary reaching out to which we respond by offering our own love, our own life, our own part in the spread of the love and light of God.

Jesus needs us still. God trusts us with our own task, whatever that may be, no matter how tiny it may seem today, for we are part of that chain reaction first kindled at the birth of Christ

Christ came silently,
unheralded by gaudy lights
or fanfare of trumpets.

Christ came silently,
attended by worried, tired people
and star-led strangers.

Christ comes silently,
unheralded by powerful voices
or media storm.

Christ comes silently,
attended by those who pause
in the quiet night.

A prayer:

"How silently, how silently the wondrous gift is given."

We sing the words, Lord, often loudly, yet rarely pause to reflect on that silence, that quietness, which surrounded the coming of Jesus into the world so that his birth was recognised only by those who paused to look to the heavens, to reflect, to risk their own journeys to find him and to offer their praise.

Loving God and Father, in a noisy, fractious world, we confess that we often seek answers from those who speak loudly, from those who are powerful, yet your gift of eternal life comes to us through the birth of a child, relying upon the care and the love of individuals, and upon the understanding of many to share that gift of life with the world.

Be with those who you have entrusted with that sharing today, we pray, that when they feel lonely and afraid, they may know the strength and guidance of your Spirit, and know that others remember them and pray for them.

We think with gratitude of the many who are quietly sharing the love of Jesus with those around them, whether it be within a refugee camp or within the corridors of power, and all places between, whether they be assisting at the time of birth or of death, and all times in between.

And thank you that you help us, when we are feeling that we're just one voice among many, to know that what we say and do and are, is important to you, and important to the spread of the love of Jesus.

As we approach a Christmastide that may be very different, we pray your peace and your joy upon those who will be alone and those who will be travelling to meet with families, praying for all people a protection from harm, and healing for those who are in distress of body or spirit, those we hold in our hearts or hear about from friends or in the media.

Give to us all, we pray, a quietness of heart that indeed, Christ may enter in. It is in his name we pray.
Amen

Happy Christmas!

I know that icons aren't everyone's 'thing' – they weren't mine for a long time, but here is one I love and which, like all icons, invites you in, to reflect. As is common to some icons, various aspects of the story are being told at once, so here's the guided tour.

In the centre is Mary, resting on a couch with Jesus beside her in the manger, the donkey and ox or cow looking on. By tradition, they warmed the baby with their breath. A nativity icon at the Monastery of St Catherine in Sinai has a cow that appears to be smiling!

To the right, on the hillside are sheep and shepherds, one with his pipe and an angel sharing the good tidings of Jesus' birth with another.

Below to the right are the midwives washing the baby, all normal, and please don't tell me that the midwives wouldn't have seen a birth in a stable or a cave – I'm sure they'd have assisted at much worse! Above, to the left are the three wise men on horseback with angels above them pointing the way. And in the bottom left corner sits Joseph, often depicted as being in his own little cave. Here, as in some icons but not all, a shepherd is speaking with him. In some stories this shepherd is Satan in disguise, tempting him to question the virgin birth. One commentator suggests that Joseph is waiting to be allowed in to see the baby but by tradition he's pondering on all that's happened. Or perhaps, I wonder, is he planning all he has to do and worrying about it?

The scene is busy, and all these people, with the exception of the midwives, are caught up in something quite new: such things as they are experiencing have never happened to them before. Which begs the question, if this is how it was at the birth of Jesus, why are so many of us getting ourselves in a state over this Christmas being different?

It's a big question, but one suggestion may be that Christmas has acquired a ritual 'normality' in a world that is increasingly uncertain. To some extent, this has always been true, from the Medieval peasant having rare time off and a good meal at the Lord's Hall amid the winter darkness and worries, but maybe the uncertainties of the present moment are making us want to hang on to our own rituals and meetings more tightly than usual. But look again at the chaos of the icon. They all coped – so can we! Jesus was born for us, God with us, and that turned people's lives upside down, and still does – in the nicest possible way!

The Christmas gift that's awkward (impossible, actually) to wrap, but that keeps on giving.

Those of us who are older (and some who are younger) will know that Christmas doesn't always work out the way we thought it should. I think my weirdest Christmas was probably ten years ago when there had been heavy snowfall, I was in the middle of a course of chemotherapy, the outlet pipe from my combi-boiler froze and an engineer wasn't able to come out until after Christmas. That was definitely an interesting one and, hey, it was fine!

Take a moment to think back to the Christmases that have been chaotic or just plain awful . . . and those that have been warm and special or perhaps hilarious. They are all part of life, have become part of who we are. Then reread Luke 2:1-7, the uncertainty of it all for Mary and Joseph.

A prayer:

Living, loving God our Father, we praise and thank you for your gift beyond all price and beyond all our deserving, the gift of Jesus your Son, gift of your own love.

We offer to you this time of celebration of the birth of Jesus, different, perhaps from years gone by, but constant in its expression of your love for us and ours for you.

We bring before you, loving Father, those who are struggling with depression and despair, those who are afraid as they think about being alone, and we bring those who are afraid as they think of the violence they know will erupt in the course of the holiday. Loving Lord, we pray safety for them, we pray your peace, the peace Christ brings, to enter all hearts.

We pray safety, too, for those who will be travelling on Christmas Day, having to hurry to fit everything into one day, perhaps tired, anxious – by your Spirit, Lord, guide them, calm them and bring them away and home safely.

Conscious that many will not be able to meet together to worship either because the church is closed, or because they are hesitant to attend for fear of the virus, we pray that they may still be aware of your love enfolding them, and aware, too, that others pray for them and that their own prayers are gifts shared, treasured.

Jesus came into a world that was busy and, in many ways, as confused and troubled as is ours. We pray for those who have great decisions to make, decisions that will affect many, that they may be guided by your Spirit into truth, into a realisation of the full implications of all they debate and decide.

As Jesus came to bring your kingdom of justice and peace, may these be the watchwords for all that is decided and enacted, and one day may your peace fill all corners of the world.

In the name of Jesus, Prince of Peace, who came to us as a baby, and is with us for all eternity, we offer these and all our prayers.

Amen

'The light shines in the darkness, and the darkness has not overcome it.' John 1:5

May this Christmas bring peace, joy and much blessing to you.

Happy new year!

My childhood was spent in Low Fell, Gateshead, living on what was then the far southern edge of the town. I remember lying in bed on New Year's Eve in the 1950s, listening to the doors opening as the men came out ahead of midnight, hearing them greet one another, "So she's thrown you out too!" and chatting and then, at midnight, loudly or softly depending on the direction of the wind, would come the sound of every ship on the quayside (and at that time the Newcastle quayside was lined with ships) all hooting to greet the New Year. At this signal, the men would shake hands and wish one another Happy New Year, then return to their homes to recite the formula that went with the symbolic gifts they brought to bring good fortune to the household in the coming year – a box of matches (light), a piece of coal (heat), a coin (money), a piece of cake (food), a glass of something (drink). Some went visiting, but mainly that was it, a remainder and reminder of the wider 'First-footing' that was deemed essential to ensure a good future. Of course, by tradition the man shouldn't be redheaded, though by this time no-one really bothered, but your first-foot absolutely must not enter the house empty-handed or bad luck would follow!

As the years passed, less and less men came out to follow the ritual, and fireworks, rather than the joyous hooting of ships, signalled midnight. The old habits died, and traffic on the Tyne declined.

Much later, in my own flat in Ouston, near Birtley, I remember just after midnight hearing the cat-flap going as the black tom-cat who lived further along the street and was thrown out each night, came in to curl up politely in a corner of my living room and snooze the night away. Being first-footed by a black cat was an interesting thought! He came empty-pawed, too.

Along with all this was the belief that everything had to be as right as it could be when midnight struck; the house clean and outstanding tasks completed, or you'd be in a state of chaos all year. The acceptance is there that some things carry over, and you can choose what they might be. That's an important truth: our past shapes our future.

Yes, 2020 has been a harsh year, and we hope that the coming year will be better, but though we have these hopes, we're also aware that the virus is no respecter of dates, and that there are changes ahead for us all as Brexit becomes reality.

Several of the Psalms tackle this issue: they recall the everlasting love of God and the way in which he has led and saved the people, and the way they have drifted away, sinned and been forgiven. Psalm 106 is one such. Or look at St. Paul, the number of times he recalls his own past, his persecution of Jesus' followers (eg. Acts 22:3-8), his ignominious escape from Damascus (2 Corinthians 11:32-3) – his past has shaped who he now is. Our past shapes us, too.

2020 has been a year in which we have struggled but also learned. As a friend said to me, we've found that we don't need to be rushing here and there, 'doing', good though that doing might have been. We have perhaps learned to value our own homes and neighbours. The small things of life have gained significance for us. Many have learned to handle and appreciate technology. The good things we've learned we can take with us into the future. The rest, and the future itself, we entrust to God.

At the millennium, we had a watchnight service at Christchurch, Halton, Leeds, where I was Minister. At midnight we went outside to sing the hymn, 'This, this is the God we adore' ('How good is the God we adore' in Rejoice and Sing). It's the second verse that says it all:

> 'Tis Jesus the first and the last
> whose Spirit shall guide us safe home;
> we'll praise him for all that is past
> and trust him for all that's to come.
>
> Joseph Hart (1712-1767)

Can you think of five things to be thankful for in the past year? And five things you pray for the coming year – for the world? for you?

A prayer:

Living God and Father of all, we face the future, one that is
uncertain, one that perhaps worries us in a way that we've not
worried before, but one in which we hope, for we hope and
trust in you.

By your Spirit, you have led us, guided us, given insight when we
have needed it, and your Spirit is with us still. Holy Spirit of
God, fill us, we pray that we may know your wisdom in these
days ahead. Through your Son Jesus, you have filled our lives
with your love, enabled us to share that love, when it has been
needed, and Jesus is with us still. Lord Jesus, may we know your
love most deeply in these days ahead.

God behind us in the past;
Christ before us, the way ahead.
Christ beside us in this moment;
Christ beneath us in our weakness;
Christ between us to bind us in the unity of his love;
Christ in us, equipping us with his all-sufficient grace. *

We bring those working in the NHS, those who are already very
tired, yet work on to bring help and comfort. Be their strength,
we pray, and be guide to those who seek to understand and
control this and other viruses. Lord, we hope and trust in you.

We bring those in nations already racked by poverty, for whom
the Lockdown has brought starvation and terrible loss. Help us
to know what to do and pray for them, we earnestly ask, as
these and all our prayers we offer in the name of Jesus, he who
brings new, hopeful life for all, this and every day.
Lord, we hope and trust in you. Amen

*section adapted from a prayer © Ian Cowie in
Hay and Stardust, compiled 2005 Ruth Burgess.

The best-laid plans . . .

Matthew 2: 1-12

The Feast of the Epiphany falls on the 6th January, when we remember the coming of the magi, the wise men, to Jesus, the first revelation of Jesus to Gentile people. It's a story I love and have thought about a great deal, even to the extent of writing my own 'take' on the tale after travel in the desert made me rethink our traditional views of their journey,* but in that work I didn't pursue the journey back home. I wonder about it now.

Imagine their initial planning: "We'll get ourselves a reliable guide, keep up a good pace and ask around when we get there – local ruler's obvious, isn't he? – find the child, spend a bit of time there maybe learning a bit about him, then take it easy coming back – look into some places we missed on the way out? Sound good?" But, as Robert Burns said, "the best-laid schemes o' mice and men gang oft a-gley." (poem, 'To a Mouse')

The reality was that they had to set off for home fairly quickly "by another route," perhaps a slow, roundabout route that would give Joseph time to arrange the family's own sudden journey to Egypt before Herod got suspicious and set his soldiers to come a-calling. Plans all gone frighteningly awry.

T.S. Eliot imagines their thoughts as they journey home in his poem, "*The Journey of the Magi*," seeing them as unsure what they had seen: a birth, yes, but also a death – a beginning or an end - they had seen them as separate, but now they wonder, as they also seriously question the life to which they return, and whether they can go on as before.

We're in a good position to really sympathise, for what became of our own plans last year? What plans we had for Christmas went suddenly adrift, we hear of couples choosing wedding dates for the fourth time and as for holidays, well! So, what do we think as we look at our own plans and hopes pre-Lockdown, the things we've lost and gained as we've journeyed through this time?

We could, of course, just want everything to be like it was, but I suspect that the whole experience of having our lives limited, our plans knocked aside can have a good outcome, if we, like Eliot's magi, reflect on it all as we go. We are probably already learning what is most precious to us, the people and the little things that maybe we took for granted before but that we now see are really important - vital even – to us.

We have all taken a journey that we didn't plan – indeed, we're on it still! It's a journey that has much to teach us, if we're open to learn. May the Holy Spirit guide our reflecting and living in these days to come so that we can look at our own lives, knowing and understanding what is precious to us as if seeing it all for the first time.

We picture the magi as kings, or if not royal, then certainly upper-class and a bit posh, yet early depictions show them in ordinary dress. If we imagine the magi as people just like us, perhaps that can help us see that their struggles connect to ours and that their determination in seeking Jesus can be ours, too.

A prayer:

> Loving God, Father, this journey through the Lockdown is hard. We had plans, we had hopes a year ago and they seem to have been tossed aside, lost. It's so easy to become despondent and wonder when this journey will end, especially when the virus proves more adaptable than we are.
>
> Thank you for the persistence of those who seek to find cures, for the skills of those who have worked on the vaccines and the skills of those who care for the sick lovingly and often at personal cost. Thank you for their acceptance of a calling that we can so easily take for granted but that is essential.
>
> We remember with thanksgiving those who have helped us: doctors, nurses, dentists, carers, radiologists, pharmacists,

auxiliary staff, cleaners and folk in administration who keep the processes of healthcare moving – for all these and more, we give thanks and praise.

Help us to be willing to make our own sacrifices so that the health of others may not be compromised.

As we reflect on the journey of the magi back to their home, we are conscious that many are kept from home or from the people who are 'home' for them. We thank you for the several ways we have of contacting family and friends, and for how much those connections mean to us. We pray for those dear to us, close at hand or far away, asking blessings and peace of heart.

We are also conscious that for many the Lockdown has led to the last journey home, home to you as they move beyond that horizon we call death. Thank you for those who have enriched our life journey but are no longer physically with us: those who gave tirelessly of themselves that others' lives may be rich.

We pray for those who mourn the loss of people they love, asking for them a real peace of heart and the touch of the love of Jesus who led the way through death to eternal life. To him we entrust those we love and to him we entrust our own life journey.

Loving, living Lord, by your Spirit guide us on this new stage of our own life journey, we pray, that we may see and understand all that you have to show us, and may live fully in each moment.

We ask it in Jesus' name.
Amen

*The little book is *A Dead Mans Gift*

Don't Dither!

© Helen E Gordon

Usually the theme for these thoughts comes easily, but this week has been difficult, not because there wasn't enough happening but because there was too much! The invasion of Capitol Hill in the US, Brexit, the to and fro about Lockdown and vaccination . . . I found myself dithering, which is an accusation that's being thrown around about the behaviour of our Prime Minister and Government and indeed about the behaviour of the US President, all in relation to COVID-19.

To some extent, one can have sympathy with the powers that be because often it's a case of you're damned if you do and damned if you don't but, as an article I read rightly said, dithering creates the worst of all possible scenarios because by the time you get round to making a decision, events have moved on and your hesitation has made the situation worse.

I believe that decision-making is made more difficult for government where there are populist leaders who don't want to look bad in the eyes of their fan base. Understandable, but when you're in a position of leadership, great or small, sometimes there are hard decisions that may make you temporarily unpopular. I was discussing this with a friend who, like me, had been a Headteacher, and she made the good point that when you were in a position of leadership, you looked at the whole picture and had to make decisions – sometimes hard ones - in that light.

This applies to parents, as leaders of their families: think how often you were annoyed at restrictions your parents put on you when you were young, only to realise later that they were right for your safety and future development as a mature adult. Or maybe you had parents who vacillated – no you can't, oh well, yes you can – and know the insecurity that can engender. And what about churches, the guidance leaders have to give? Do we put off, dither?

The story of St Paul's shipwreck comes to mind, Acts 27:4-44. Paul, a prisoner along with other prisoners was being taken by sea to Rome via Crete, late in the year when the chance of shipwreck, as Paul pointed out, was high. The owner of the ship and the Captain argued for carrying on, I suspect with commercial gain the motivating factor. (Sound familiar?) After an easy start, the wind changed and things began to go very badly. Paul encouraged them, after a bit of 'I told you so', but then it seems that the Captain wasn't in full control of his crew, because the sailors tried to abandon ship. Paul persuaded the soldiers to take decisive action and cut the ropes holding the life-boats, making it all or nothing for everyone. Then the ship ran aground and the soldiers wanted to kill the prisoners in case they escaped, but again Paul persuaded them otherwise and organised the whole people reaching safety either swimming or floating on planks.

From chaos, Paul led the people through to safety. He had a clear vision for the future and absolute trust in God and was clear and forceful in his speaking. No populist, Paul: he had friends, he cared about people, but he didn't court a personal popularity and that enabled him to speak out boldly in hard situations.

As for us? Being alone in Lockdown certainly affects decision-making: we can easily obsess about some issues and fret about others. We pray the guidance of the Holy Spirit to bring to everyone peace of mind and courage to carry on wisely through these stormy and difficult days.

In contrast to the ditherer, a Norwegian mountain that is fixed, strong. It takes battering from the wind, sea and snow yet it stands firm. Through these difficult times when we are cut off from much that sustains us – friends, family, church – and are battered by fears, pray that we stand firm, making good decisions, calmly.

A prayer:

Lord our God, who was and is and is to come, we seek you. You hold all wisdom: through your Spirit you bring clarity. You hold all love: through your Son Jesus, you demonstrate its height and depth. In times when we are directionless, when there seem several good options and several bad ones, we ask that same wisdom to see the way forward. In times when we are uncertain, when what we believe and what others say is in conflict, we ask that same wisdom to see the way forward.

In times when we are certain of our own rightness, when the future direction seems clear, we ask that same wisdom and humility to make us pause and seek your calm before we act.

Lord, the times in which we live are full of uncertainty. We ask the wisdom of the Holy Spirit for all in positions of leadership, especially our own Government in their dealing with the Pandemic, Brexit and immigration. Help all in government, we pray, to seek a true way forward that will bring healing to the nations, and to act decisively in ways that will bring peace.

Lord, our churches are full of uncertainty, some fearful they will never reopen, all aware that the future will not necessarily be easy. We ask the love of Jesus to fill all, as we seek to share that love in new ways, through the Internet, through phone calls and FaceTime, and as we share that love through our prayers. Keep us always faithful in prayer, Lord.

We pray for those who are ill, and for those who care for them – for the NHS at this stressed and difficult time . . . and for those who have hard decisions to make with finite resources . . . we pray, too, for those in less developed nations where COVID-19 has added to huge stresses . . . where vaccinating people brings problems of cost and management . . . we ask wisdom, we ask peace and a just sharing of resources.

Lord our God, who was and is and is to come, you hold us all in your love and wisdom. Hear our prayer, we ask, in Jesus name.

Amen

It's not Magic!

Someone on Radio 4 last week observed that from the start of the Pandemic, the Government has been looking for a magic bullet against it, the vaccine having become this magic bullet.

I am inclined to agree with him. From the beginning, the tone has veered between honest looking at the facts and a reassurance that somehow didn't reassure all of us. Initially, it was stressed that COVID-19 was of greatest danger to the elderly, 'an old people's ilness' even, and indeed, elderly people who catch it are most likely to be seriously ill or die, especially when they have other underlying conditions. Some of we elderly, while accepting the truth of that last statement, were sceptical that the virus only had us in its sights, and now the new strain is affecting all ages – also on Radio 4 was a doctor saying that half his patients in ICU are now under 50 years old. And then there is the vaccine. Hold on the vaccine is coming! Hold on, the vaccine is here and we'll be able to go back to normal life!

An article in the 'News' app on my phone titled "Vaccines alone aren't enough to eradicate a virus – lessons from history," reminds readers that it was not vaccination alone that eradicated various ills of the past –

smallpox, for example - but vaccination alongside other technological developments and a spread of vaccination throughout the world, and that it took a long time. Sadly, today many see science, or specifically medicine, as a kind of magic that can cure all things almost instantly, without us making any changes to our lives and, sorry folks, that just isn't true.

I know this in my own life. Ten years ago when I had biopsies taken for Hodgkins Lymphoma, breast cancer cells – the type I had had in 1992 – were found and for the last ten years the cancer has been present but at so low a level that it didn't show on scans. Some relatives of mine found that unbelievable. "But surely there must be some scan that would show it?" No. Medicine is not magic!

I'm reminded of Peter and Jesus, when Peter had just grasped the truth that Jesus was the Messiah and said it out loud (Matthew 16:13-23). No doubt, in Peter's mind, that truth pointed to a joyful future when everything would come right, so we can understand his horror when Jesus began talking about the suffering ahead, speaking even of his death. He rebuked Jesus – "God forbid it, Lord! This must never happen to you." – and Jesus absolutely bawled him out. "You are a stumbling block to me." There would be no magic, no fantastical rescue from the inevitable human order of things. Resurrection, amazing new life was to come, but not before a harsh time in which Jesus needed the disciples to stay faithful and tough it out with him. They weren't so good at the toughing it out bit, but they did stay around, and that faithfulness, even when they were confused and not knowing, was all-important for the future.

I believe this applies to the present moment. Yes, we will come out of

Photograph taken near Stanley Crook, winter of 2008-9

all this, but not in a flash. The vaccine is a massive blessing, but we have to play our part in being sensible even when others aren't, hard though we may find it, and it is hard now, when we are weary almost a year from the first Lockdown. The hard slog is always the most wearying; to change the metaphor, when I did a lot of serious walking I always preferred the steep scramble to the steady climb that seemed to go on and on for ever. But it didn't go on for ever and it doesn't.

Stay faithful; tough it out – and pause to find blessing even in this present moment.

From the hymn "'Tis winter now"

> 'O God, you give the winter's cold,
> as well as summer's joyous rays,
> you warmly in your love enfold
> and keep us through life's wintry days.'
>
> Samuel Longfellow (1819-1892)

A prayer:

Loving God and Father, in whom is light and the warmth of profound love, we come to you in this wintery time seeking that warmth, a reassurance of your presence. It is hard when it is cold and slippery outside: the streets that have felt unsafe because of COVID-19, can now feel unsafe because of ice and slush, wind and rain. We are trapped inside, and somehow that's good because it's warm and safe, but somehow also bad, because we feel restricted, unmotivated. When we talk to others on the phone, we have little news to share. Even praying becomes difficult. Forgive our inertia, we ask.

By your Spirit, give us resilience and hope to be the best we can be and to do all we can in these strange times. Help us all to remember those in nations far poorer than our own where buying sufficient vaccine would be impossible, and those nations where governments choose who will receive and who not, according to wealth and not need.

And help us, we pray, to act with thought for one another in all we do and say. We pray strength, peace and safety for those working in health care, continuing to provide for the sick and frightened, and for all involved in the mass vaccination.

We pray, too, for those who have kept working hard throughout and often subject to abuse – shop assistants, those delivering all we order online, postal workers and so many more, unsung, often unnoticed. Lord, we pray a blessing upon them.

We pray for those who are sick at this time . . . and those whose life has become unsafe, at home with abusive partners, parents or children . . . hold them in your love, shield them with your strength, guide them in ways of safety and healing.

At this time of Prayer for Christian Unity, we bring the churches of our local communities, seeking your blessing for them in all they may be doing to share the Gospel today. May the love of Christ fill them and spill out into the world around, for we ask it in Jesus' name, he who suffered pain and death itself for the salvation of the world.

Amen

Peril and Possibility

For the first time ever I watched the inauguration of the US President, and this phrase in his address sprang out at me: "this winter of peril and significant possibility." I wondered, does peril inevitably bring with it possibility? And how do we find the possibility amid the peril?

In September 1839 a four-year scientific expedition to the Antarctic set out under the leadership of Captain James Clark Ross in HMS Erebus, her sister ship, HMS Terror being captained by Commander Francis Crozier, Ross' long-time colleague and friend. Both men were experienced and respected seamen, used to polar waters and travelling arctic lands. Ross had been first to discover the location of magnetic north and was understandably keen to get the set.

Within two years they had discovered 'The Great Icy Barrier' (now Ross Ice Shelf), closing off hope of reaching magnetic south; however, they had by then sailed further south than any other ship and been first to see the awesome sight of a volcano and mountain beyond the barrier, which Ross named Erebus and Terror respectively.

The second season of exploration closing, on the night of February 13th March 1842, they found themselves in a heavy sea headed for a chain of cliff-like icebergs. Attempting to avoid these, the ships collided: their rigging became entangled and damaged, the next wave disentangled the rigging but lifted the ships to crash down on one another. Peril is an understatement.

Crozier spotted a gap between the bergs and got Terror through what proved to be a very narrow channel to calm water (it could easily have been a dead end). Erebus was badly damaged, and Ross decided to 'make a sternboard' – to drive the ship backwards, as far as I understand to redirect it, a hugely hazardous act in heavy seas, but it worked, yardarm scraping the face of the iceberg and the whole stern plunging underwater. He was then able to guide the ship to safety.

It's interesting that in all the accounts, praise is given to God for their saving, and indeed, at daybreak they saw that the chain of icebergs spread for miles, with the only gap being the one they'd come through. Marine Sergeant Cunningham on Terror, wrote, "it was a most wonderful interposition of Divine providence that we were not all Sent into the presence of our Maker." A miracle indeed. Ross and Crozier, both devout men, led services of thanksgiving.

In great peril, possibility seen and action taken, action that arose from long experience and the fulfilling of which required immense trust – the trust of the two leaders in each other and the trust of the men in their leaders. Yes, the crews had been chosen for this expedition and were used to obeying orders, but it's clear that respect was high, Ross writing glowingly of the way in which the men "ran up the rigging with as much alacrity as on any ordinary occasion."

Respect, trust and faith – these are surely what we all need in our life, the life of the church no less than life social and political, a respect, trust and faith that needs to be built up in normal time so that in time of peril, we might find the possibility of a safe route home. I don't think I can do better than leave the last words to John Davis, Second Master of Terror, who noted in a letter home, "I cried with the Psalmist, "Oh, Lord, teach us to number our days that we may apply our hearts unto wisdom." (Psalm 90.)

Sailors' words are quoted in M.J. Ross, Ross in the Antarctic. 1982 Caedmon of Whitby.

The icebergs in the Antarctic are cliff-like, as compared to the stepped icebergs of northern regions. Some time later, peril long past, both captains found their hands shaking uncontrollably – Post Traumatic Stress Disorder, methinks. The Polar Gallery of the National Maritime Museum in Greenwich has pictures painted by John Davis, including "Erebus passing through the Chain of Bergs." Worth a visit.

A prayer:

Lord our God and Father, in this "winter of peril and significant possibility" many are afraid. Afraid of the Lockdown, afraid of the heedlessness of some, afraid for the future of young people, we seem to be tossed hither and thither. Each also has their own fears for themselves, for family, for friends, for the state of the world, and in the night-time these fears rise up like great cliffs before them and there seems no way of escape.

Yet with you in calm, is safety, is true guidance and with the Psalmist we can say, "My refuge and my fortress; my God in whom I trust" * Lord, indeed we trust in you, in the love of Jesus and the guidance of your Spirit, and in that trust we live our lives, seeking to do your will as we use the gifts and abilities you have given us for the good of all.

We are conscious of the need for trust in those who lead us, whether in society or the Church, and pray for all who bear heavy burdens of leadership in these testing times, in government both local and national and within the Church. For them all we earnestly pray the wisdom of the Holy Spirit to fill them and guide their decisions, this we pray particularly for the United States of America at this time of change and new possibilities.

We bring those scientists who today are exploring the intricacies of so many ills that beset the world and ways of living sustainably. For them too we pray the guidance of the Holy Spirit in their research, in the conclusions they draw and in the words they speak to the public.

And for we ordinary folk, who can be in our own way and through your love and inspiration, extraordinary, we pray courage in time of peril, and the ability to live in a way that encourages others, helps others trust in the faith we share. In Jesus name we pray, he who passed through the peril of death itself to glorious new life for us.

Amen

*Psalm 91, worth reading at this time!

The Winter of the Jigsaw Puzzle!

Jigsaw puzzles have become the go-to activity for many in our confined-to-the-house state. Along with the regular jigsaw fans are new converts learning the obsessive nature of the hobby, the just seeking another piece before you go to bed, get the tea – anything! How many of you are wondering where the loose pieces will fit in the image above?

For a moment, let's look at your life as a great jigsaw that you're building up with only little glimpses of what the picture might be, wondering how bits fit together and whether you've even got all the pieces you need. That happens with actual jigsaws when you're sure, sometimes, that you don't have the piece to fit in a particular space; it's only when the puzzle is almost competed that you find the elusive piece and wonder how you ever missed it. Bit like looking back on life!

We all have different ways of tacking jigsaw puzzles. Most, if not all, start by finding and fitting the edge pieces; we set the parameters of the picture early. Next, some folk sort through all the pieces to put them in different piles by colour or shape while others, myself included, just dive straight in and work in a haphazard way, a bit like our different approaches to life itself! Mostly we look for sections to work on – a brightly coloured bit, perhaps, or an obvious image and we build that up, perhaps noticing pieces that don't fit immediately, but are worth putting aside for later. Definitely like life, that – busy with the present, we are on the lookout for future possibilities.

But when we have a few sections built up, there might seem no obvious way that they link up. It's only as the puzzle progresses that we find the connecting parts and sometimes discover that the reason we've not been able to knit them together thus far is because we made a mistake somewhere. And when an actual jigsaw is broken – someone nudges the table or the cat leaps in the middle of it – it's often in the rebuilding, (after a lot of muttering, not to say swearing) that we find the error and how the sections fit together.

Imagine, then, your life-jigsaw coming along nicely, and then the Pandemic, or any unexpected happening, seizes a corner and shakes it so hard that a great section falls apart. That's how many of us feel: that our lives have been so shaken that the plans we had, the picture we had in mind for the future, is in pieces.

At some point we will rebuild, if we haven't already begun, and in the rebuilding we may well find things fitting together differently. We might find – have already found – that what we thought was important to our life actually isn't, that our values have changed and we see our life-picture with different eyes. We might find new, vibrant, connections, with people, with faith, with nature.

St. Paul, writing to encourage the Philippian Church (Philippians 1: 20-27) said, "For to me, living is Christ and dying is gain. If I am to live in the flesh, that means fruitful labour for me; and I do not know which I prefer." Although he longed to be with Christ, he was happy to keep on putting together the pieces of his life that also helped build up the picture of the Philippians' lives, for as long as he was needed.

I'll end with suggesting you look at Psalm 139:13-18 – "Your eyes beheld my unformed substance" - God has a whole picture of each of us and will help us fit the pieces together!

I've just rediscovered an interest in tapestry work, again a building of a picture in which the colours blend and complement one another.

Things to think about: As we ask God to help us restore the picture, has the Pandemic given you a different 'take' on life? Has it caused you to rethink how you live your life? Is your picture of the future changed or changing?

A prayer:

"O Lord, you have searched me and know me," said the Psalmist. Lord God our Father, you search me and know me, and in that searching and knowing, you love me. I don't understand how or why, for so often, as I look at my life, I see where I have gone astray, failed in so many ways to be the person I want to be, the person I imagine myself to be in my better moments. Loving Lord, help me rebuild those parts of my life that are shattered and damaged.

By your Holy Spirit, guide me in truth and wisdom and compassion that I may live a creative life of peace, that helps build your Kingdom here on Earth.

The Pandemic has shaken so many lives worldwide, bringing loss of people, of loved family members, of friends, loss of livelihood. Loving Lord, your Son Jesus came into our troubled and hurting world bringing healing, and bringing peace and hope where there was none. May his love fill and inspire those who today bring comfort and healing within our hospitals, care homes and within own homes.

We thank you most earnestly for those who have unstintingly given of themselves during this Pandemic, even when they have been weary and feeling hopeless. We ask that we may never take for granted the sacrifices others make, and always keep in our prayers those who we overlook, but whose contribution to the good of the world is so vital – those who work to maintain water supplies, sewers, our refuse collectors, and so many more. In thanksgiving for their work, we pray for their safety.

We pray for those in authority, those we trust have a larger picture before them, a picture built from shared knowledge. We pray the wisdom to realise when that knowledge is partial, and the humility to seek answers beyond their own comfort zones.

And we pray for the Church in these days when the Pandemic has challenged us to seek new ways of being and of sharing the love of Christ. May we have a Spirit-inspired wisdom and humility to see what we should maintain of these new ways for your glory and the furtherance of your Kingdom.

Thank you, Lord, that you hear us, love us, guide us always as we pray in Jesus' name.

Amen

Rain, rain, go away, come again another day.

© Helen E Gordon

Thus did we used to chant as children, hopelessly. Great Britain has always been a rainy place and feels more so now, especially in the south and west. Even where I am in the east, the ground is completely saturated and we are soaked if we venture out.

Now I've said that, it'll no doubt stop raining, just as when a Minister for Drought was appointed in August 1976 after Britain's driest summer in 200 years, it immediately began to bucket down so that the poor man was nicknamed 'Minister for Rain.'

We are so used to rain in this country that it can be difficult to imagine how it feels to live through a real drought such as seized the land of Israel in the time of the prophet Elijah (1 Kings 18:1 & 17-46). They suffered, they prayed, they hoped and eventually there came a great competition on Mount Carmel between the Priests of Baal and Elijah, Prophet of God to discover whose god wielded true power. The Priests went first, praying in ever more frenzied ways for Baal to bring down fire on their sacrificed bull, while Elijah yelled rude comments from the side-lines. When they were exhausted, Elijah stepped forward, built an altar with a great ditch around it, laid the wood for the fire and the meat on the altar then poured four jars of water over it – this he repeated twice more. It's an action with long antecedents, a demonstration to the god that look, this is what we need: water. But it was also an act of terrific faith or folly to throw away so much water at a time of drought. When you are thirsty, to see water thrown on the ground actually hurts.

It was an act of faith. He prayed and down came fire that consumed the sacrifice, the wood, the stones, even the dust and all the water. Then Elijah waited, after a bit of slaughter of the priests of Baal (they were like that then). He sent his servant to look towards the sea – what did he see? Nothing. At the seventh time of looking, he saw "a little cloud, no bigger than a person's hand is rising out of the sea." "Go home," Elijah told the king, "before the rain starts hard." Wise counsel. In arid lands, a sudden heavy rainfall can cause flash flooding; the dried-up river beds (wadis) become a raging torrent within minutes and people and animals can be swept away and drowned. Water sustains life but can also bring death. And it rained.

Of course today, we question how much the changes in the seasons and the extremes of weather we experience here and abroad are a feature of global warming; how much is down to the natural eccentricities of our climate and how much is down to our greedy misuse of the earth. Realistically, science is clear that the latter is the major factor, and we have to take that on board. As Christians, we can't chant some 'God, get us out of this,' prayers and hope it's all going to be alright. We are on earth to care for creation as well as enjoying it. Adam and Eve tended the garden, don't forget, and God met with them there (Genesis 2:15 & 3:8-9). The earth matters.

But we are weary of rain (and snow) and want it to go away. We even more desperately want the virus to go away. We pray, we try to live more sustainably (our own kind of small sacrifice). And, having done all that, if we're wise, we keep a look-out for the signs of change and, like Elijah's servant, we might need to keep watching and watching until we discern that tiny, but real, sign that things are changing. Only then can we properly prepare to move forward thoughtfully and joyfully into a resumption of a more 'normal' life. Keep praying! Keep watching!

We pray, and we work. And while we do, we can always enjoy the rain! A cheerful umbrella always helps!

A prayer:

Safe under the protection of your love, we come before you. Outside that protection, the woes of the world seem to batter all beneath them – the Lockdown, fighting abroad, violence at home, flood, famine, war. Through the guiding of your Holy Spirit, help us be watchful for the signs of hope, the signs that new beginning is near, and help us continue patient, preparing for that moment in our hearts and in our lives.

Remembering the story of Elijah, we bring to mind those countries where drought is a regular feature, bringing famine and great loss. We pray strength and wisdom for those organisations and individuals who try to bring aid, who have to face distressing scenes and a frequent sense of helplessness. May they see and be encouraged by those tiny signs of hope: lives changed and saved.

Lord, we bring before you those of us who live in countries where water is plentiful, where we are comfortable, where we waste so much of the earth's resources, and ask that your Spirit may guide us, as individuals, in the decisions we make, and governments in the decisions they make that can affect so many. Help us remember that we are one people, your people.

Seeing the snow outside our windows and the water-logged earth, we bring those who are living in makeshift shelters in snow and rain: refugee families huddling together for warmth, rough sleepers on our own streets, wet and cold; and we bring those who seek to bring aid, asking safety and strength for all.

We bring, too, those who have to make decisions between having food or fuel, full stomachs against warm houses, and thinking of this, we pray for those organising and running food banks and debt counselling; for Local Authority housing officers, social workers, asking for them wisdom and strength.

And finally, we pray for all those working through Lockdown to ensure food supplies, for heating and electrical engineers, water authority engineers, and for all who work within the caring professions. Be with them, we ask, when they are especially tired: may they know that they are appreciated.

Thank you for your love, Lord, shown through the lives of so many people. Thank you for your love for each and every one.

Amen

The Season of Lent begins

I don't know about you, but Lent seems to have crept up suddenly. I hate to blame the Pandemic for everything, but I do wonder if the changed nature of our lives today might have something to do with it!

In Lent, we remember Jesus' temptations in the Wilderness (Matthew 4: 1-11) and reflect upon our own temptations - often the tendency to eat the wrong things. I guess those who've put on weight during Lockdown might find that exercise useful, but resisting temptation won't be easy when there is less to divert attention from our longings. It will involve, as it did for Jesus, a wrestling with the temptation.

Our local Ministers' Bible Study was looking at the passage in which Jacob wrestles at the ford over the River Jabbok (Genesis 32:22-31). Returning to his homeland and preparing to meet his wronged elder brother, Esau, Jacob had sent everyone across the river ahead of him and was alone when his way was barred by a man with whom he wrestled all night.

As we discussed it, the question of who won came up. And from that came the thought that so much language today is about fighting and beating whatever it is – we fight illness, we fight depression, we fight - and I wonder, is it wrestling, not fighting, that we really need to be doing?

When we are faced with something that bars our way forward – illness, bereavement, this Pandemic – we can choose to run from it, to fight against it, or to wrestle with it, understand it, see its strengths and weaknesses, and finally come to an accommodation with it. This latter option isn't easy, as it means living with uncertainty for longer than is altogether comfortable, but it can enable us to live more fully.

My mother's father had a serious heart condition that had led to him take early retirement. After my grandmother died, he returned to his hometown of Pickering where he lived a long and active life, walking or cycling in the countryside, often alone. If his heart played up, he would lie by the roadside until he felt better and then continue. Over the years, he had come to understand and live with his heart's limitations and strengths and with that knowledge, lived into his eighties.

Neither side conceded when Jacob wrestled, and he was injured but then given a blessing by his opponent, and a new name, Israel. Then Jacob realised "I have seen God face to face, and yet my life is preserved." He left the confrontation with new insight but also with pain; as we wrestle

with whatever lies before us – illness, loss of many kinds including loss of hope, or maybe we face difficult people, or a change of direction – we can be given new insight.

Perhaps this Lent might be an opportunity to wrestle with where we are and, indeed, who we are now, how the Pandemic might have changed us, our hopes and fears for the future, our attitudes and above all, where God is in all of this. Remember, it was through the wrestling that Jacob realised the presence of God. It's worth the struggle for, although we may come out of it limping, like Jacob, we will be blessed.

One way to tackle temptation is to look ahead to where we want to be and how we want to be. Then you ask, will what you're doing or are temped to do help or hinder you?

A prayer:

Lord, it is hard, this wrestling. We want to walk away – run, even – from hard things that face us, or we want to beat them back so that they vanish, but deep within, we know this isn't the way. Thank you that Jesus faced temptation to do and be something you didn't want of him; the temptation to take the easy way out, to go the powerful, popular route. He wrestled with these temptations and overcame them. May we, in his name and in his strength, overcome our own temptations and problems.

We pray for all those who are in any kind of position of authority and who have to struggle with the temptation to seize personal power rather than seeking the good of all people, and we ask a special insight and strength for those who challenge such grasping of power, especially where power has been grasped with subtlety and craftiness.

We pray for all who are wrestling today with their own temptations, great and small, asking for them the wisdom to know when they are struggling for right ways forward, and strength to persevere. May your Spirit guide and the love of Christ motivate.

Thank you for the reminder, Lord, that after he had wrestled with temptation, in the midst of the wilderness angels ministered to Jesus. Thank you that your messengers minister to us when we are deeply in need, giving us an inner strength and peace when both seem so unlikely, bringing to us people who will help by their words and action and by just being there, firm and settled, when we need to rely on their strength and calm.

Thank you especially at this time for nurses, doctors and all working in our hospitals, clinics and surgeries; district nurses, midwives, and paramedics, health workers and carers who come into our homes, sometimes facing awful situations with a quiet efficiency. Be with them, we pray, and may they find others who will give them the love and understanding they need when their minds and hearts are full of troubles.

Thank you, too, that Jacob emerged from the night of wrestling with a new name, and blessed. May we be aware of the blessing and new beginning you give us, even within the darkest times. May our minds and hearts be open today to that blessing, as we ask it in Jesus' name.

Amen

A Road Map

Many people struggle with maps, and the way forward can seem blank. But with the popularity of Sat-navs, fewer people carry road maps in their cars and even fewer are learning how to read maps, or even notice signs, all of which makes it interesting that the Prime Minister has used the metaphor of a road map to lead out of Lockdown. My cynical self thinks that a plan for getting out of a maze might be a better choice, but a road map it is.

I confess that I'm no great map reader when asked to navigate on a journey – I belong to that maligned group of people who sometimes need to turn the map upside-down to see the direction of travel – but I get there in the end.

However, getting there in the end is relatively easy when you have a definite destination, when you know exactly on the map where you are, have a clear plan which roads you want to follow, and are aware of possible alternatives. Planning a route out of Lockdown is surely a very different matter, when knowing exactly where we are in terms of cases, deaths, vaccination is variable and there must be a vast array of possible routes, not to mention a vast array of advice from interested parties. We are not following a road map so much as creating a complex new one.

I wrote a few weeks ago about Sir James Clarke Ross' exploration of the Antarctic in 1839-43. His, and others', voyages were mapping as they went and a difficulty they faced was the phenomenon known as 'ice blink', a mirage created when the sun reflects on the ice to create an impression of land or mountain ranges in the distance. The best of explorers fell victim to this, and so Ross marked with a dotted line 'land' that had not been verified as such. There's a nice description of the ships' rigging crowded with officers and crew looking out for an island drawn in by another explorer and which they concluded – when they'd sailed through it a few times – never existed.

In a way we are in the same position with regard to emerging from the Pandemic. There is much good advice from scientists, but the way forward isn't as clear as we'd like, things turn out to be not exactly as they seemed and we have learned that the virus is far more adaptable than we are.

In the Church, when we begin to emerge from Lockdown and from the restrictions laid upon us, we will be faced with questions. There has been experimentation that has worked, for example services on Zoom have been a positive experience for many (meetings too) and I have heard of highly successful drive-in services. To go back to the road map metaphor, new roads have been explored and found to be good. Do we ignore these when we are free to meet as before and let the new routes fall into disrepair? Perhaps those new routes might prove important in the future, so to lose them would seem a pity. Jesus' words come to mind:

"Therefore every scribe who has been trained for the kingdom of heaven is like the master of a household who brings out of his treasure what is new and what is old."

(Matthew 13:52).

Moving forward as society and as church can seem daunting at the present moment, but maybe it's time to recognise that the way we've had to live for the past year will have changed us in some ways and that we are now mapping new routes that draw on this experience as well as on our traditions. Given that, maybe it's time to be brave and embrace the future with hope and joy, for we don't journey alone: Christ is with us always, the Spirit our guide.

"I am with you always, to the end of the age."

(Matthew 28:20)

A prayer:

With the Psalmist we pray:
"Make me to know your ways, O Lord, teach me your paths.
Lead me in the truth and teach me, for you are the God of my
salvation: for you I wait all day long."   (Psalm 25: 4-5)

Eternal Lord God and Father, you have watched over humanity
through the ages, through times when pathways have been clear
and times when the way ahead has been puzzling, uncertain.

In Jesus you have shown us the depth and height of your love;
your commitment to us, and in his name we bring our prayers
confidently, knowing that we are heard and understood.

But we are also aware that you have watched over us through times we have gone badly astray. Collectively, we have wrought destruction upon each other and upon the earth. Individually, we have nourished the thoughts, words and deeds that are at the root of such destruction. We beg your forgiveness for our collective and individual sins and faults, those committed knowingly and those committed thoughtlessly.

May we live as people forgiven and restored, enabled to forge new roadways of hope, of understanding and peace, through the guidance of your Holy Spirit.

We pray for the Church, that we may always seek the mind of Christ in all we do and say, and be unafraid when faced by new ways to share the Gospel. Help us draw wisely from old and new to the furtherance of your Kingdom.

To the coming of your Kingdom we look with joy. Guide us in right pathways, guide us in right words to say, ever guide us in your ways of justice and peace. Thank you, Lord, that you hear us as we pray, now and always.

Amen

Both images © Catherine Richardson.

Signs of Spring

Just as we see signs that day is breaking – a lightening of the sky on the distant horizon, a chill in the air – before the sun actually rises, so we see signs of spring before it is officially with us. The first day of spring, my diary tells me, is 20th March, but spring is all around us, and I suspect that global warming is playing havoc with our traditional seasons anyway.

It gives an uplift to see these early signs – the snowdrops, the crocuses and now even daffodils – those indications that a colourful and joyous life begins again. But we know that spring weather can be unpredictable and sometimes treacherous, and we fear for the new-born lambs in the fields, the emerging flowers.

This is probably why our symbols of spring are quite tough. I remember the first time I felt a lamb's woolly coat and found the soft fluffy appearance disguised a tough, dense coat, the outer hairs hard and curved to make a waterproof covering over the warm inner. The bulbs that leap to flower in early spring are likewise hardy, emerging from a covering of snow as fresh as ever. I was recently told that Bumblebee queens who emerge from hibernation early in the year are also tough. They all have to be.

The signs of new life do not mean that everything will now be sunny and easy. Signs of emergence from the Lockdown do not mean that everything immediately goes back to how it was before. Spring can be a hard, confusing time of sunshine and cold, peril and hope, but a time we have to live through before summer comes.

But there is a human aspect to spring. Some years ago I saw a lay preacher begin his children's address by showing us a bag and asking if we could guess what sign of spring was inside it. We went through all the usual stuff – flowers, rabbit, Easter eggs - then like a conjuror pulling a rabbit from a hat he took from the bag . . . a tin of paint. Spring cleaning.

In faith terms, spring is also a time of 'cleaning', of reflecting on our lives and how we live them. Surely it should also be a time of nurturing the good within each of us, the strengths God has given us so that we can weather the storms, actual and emotional. St Paul wrote these encouraging words: "No testing has overtaken you that is not common to everyone. God is faithful, and he will not let you be tested beyond your strength, but with the testing he will also provide the way out so that you may be able to endure it" (1 Corinthians 10:13).

We have been through – are still in - a very testing time, and many of us are very weary. The ups and downs of emergence from the Lockdown increase our longings for all that will come, for our own summer time, and those longings are different for each one, and run very deep. It may even be that the signs of spring feel almost hurtful, the newness reminding us of our losses.

Perhaps a reminder of God's promise that came with the sign of the rainbow is what we need:

"As long as the earth endures, seedtime and harvest, cold and heat, summer and winter, day and night, shall not cease" (Genesis 8: 22). We give thanks for the beauty of the present moment and for the promised time to come, which will in time bring its own special blessings.

Something to think about: What qualities do you have that have helped you cope? These have been a gift from God. What are your great longings as you look ahead to the summer? These will be a gift from God. What gives you most joy as you look around you and within yourself? This is a gift from God. Give thanks!

A prayer:

Eternal, living Lord, thank you that you have given to each of us the strength to cope with all we have had to face in life thus far. Some of the hardships we have faced, in everyday living and in our emotional being, have left us tired or even exhausted and there have been times we've only just coped. These times can feel very lonely, Lord.

Help us see, in the signs of spring, signs of the new life you offer us, and in them find hope and strength. Thank you for the great sign of your love, the rainbow, that promise of continuing life, and thank you especially for that sign of your eternal love, Jesus, your Son, who in his living, dying and rising again has assured us of true, eternal life. For this we praise and glorify you, confident in the faithfulness of Jesus.

We praise you, too, for the gift of the Holy Spirit, through whose work we are able to discern that which is hopeful and joyful in the world, and see ways forward so that we can live fully to the furtherance of the Kingdom of God, the Kingdom of peace.

Hold in your love, we ask, those who look about them and see only reminders of everything they have lost, those who fear the future. We bring those who are tender in faith, those who struggle to accept your love in Jesus, asking for them the guiding of the Spirit. We bring those who are tender in physical and mental health, asking for them your healing and your peace, and alongside we bring with thanksgiving those who work with the ill, the disadvantaged.

We bring those who work to find ways forward out of all the change the Lockdown has wrought, asking for them the wisdom of the Spirit. We bring those at home and abroad working the land, that they may be guided in wisdom, and upheld when weary.

Give to us all eyes to see the wonder of renewing life about us, we pray. And hearts warm to care for that new life in nature and in the people about us, for we ask it in the name of Jesus, whose love is new and living each day.

Amen

A Special Day!

Last week I was the recipient of a surprise bouquet of flowers from my nieces. The accompanying card said, "Here is a gift to let you know we are thinking about you and missing you! Happy Auntie Day!" The "Happy Auntie Day!" reminded me of a silly thought I had years ago in response to a proliferation of special 'days' for this one and that. What about a Day for Solitary People with No Friends? Realistically, I couldn't see the card manufacturers getting on board with a no-friends card. The one you would really rather not get!

And then Disney's Alice in Wonderland came to mind, the part where the Mad Hatter and March Hare tell Alice that they're celebrating their unbirthdays. You only get one birthday a year, they explain, but you have 364 unbirthdays. (Or 365 in a Leap Year.) Then they sing the song, "A very merry unbirthday to me." Actually, Googling the words, I discover that there's a whole range of unbirthday cards and even, believe it or not, cards (some quite mean) for the friendless. I give up. There are no depths commerce will not plumb.

However, making each day a special day is no bad idea - though no tea party, mad or otherwise, please! - and it has a particular resonance just now when each day kind of merges into the next, unchanging, whereas pre-Lockdown, life had a rhythm to it. If we look further back, there was even more of a set pattern – a washing day, a shopping day, a baking day. Interestingly, those of us who were disorganised now find ourselves falling into set routines. For me, Monday is completing and sending off this work, Tuesday or Wednesday going into Durham to put up the posters and do shopping on the way home. Sunday is Zoom service day.

Sunday. The seventh day in which God rested, according to the Genesis account of Creation which, though not a Creationist myself, never ceases to intrigue me in the way in which the Genesis account broadly agrees with the evolutionary sequence of creation.

It's an account divided into particular events on particular days (Genesis 1: 1-31), and each day has its particular glory; "And God saw that it was good" is repeated at the close of most days. Even in these Lockdown days, it's worth pausing each night to look back and see what has been good and perhaps unique in the day. It could be something quite small, something we've seen or read, something we've felt, a phone call made or received. Something that made us laugh.

Then perhaps we can plan to make each day special. A meal to look forward to. A book to read. A programme to watch or listen to. A phone call to make, perhaps to someone we've not contacted for ages. It might be a good time for the more sociable among us to look through our Christmas card list or through some old photographs and make contact with an old friend and make their day special. It can seem a bit trite to say that each day is special, a gift from God, but it's nevertheless true, and what we do with that gift is down to us.

Then, sometimes, what we would have seen as mundane now stands out for us – a visit to the dentist or a hospital appointment perhaps, and we dress up for it and think we're being a bit foolish. Why? The dentist or doctor might well appreciate that we've made the effort! And you'll feel better for making that day a bit different. Special. Then rest, give thanks, and put your feet up!

Enjoy the earth. Enjoy each day, for each day is special. Why? Why not? And happy unbirthday to you!

Jesus said, "I came that they may have life, and have it abundantly."
(John 10:10)

A prayer:

Creative, living Lord God, who looked and looks upon the earth and all within it and sees that it is good, we pause in wonder at the glory of that creation. The skies above, the ground beneath our feet in its multiplicity of colours.The creatures, large and small, whether ugly or beautiful to us. The people around us, whether known or unknown, old or young, smiling or frowning. Everything has the potential to reflect your glory, the wonder of your being.

We praise you and thank you, Lord God our Father, for our own potential to reflect that glory. We are conscious that all is not well within your creation. Earth and seas and now even space are polluted through our own carelessness and greed. The same greed, and our possessiveness, creates conflict, war, in which the innocent, people and the earth itself, suffer.

All this we mourn and long for change. We long for a world in which people can live in peace, a world in which nature flourishes. Forgive us, individually and collectively, we pray, the action and inaction that so mars creation.

Within the world, many are fearful, each day one to be faced with dread. We bring to mind and thus before you, Lord, those who feel trapped within their homes, afraid to venture out. We bring those caught in abusive relationships made worse by the close confinement of Lockdown. We bring those fearful of the future, whether they will have work, enough money, a home.

And we bring those who have the power to make changes: those in government, finance and industry, that they might be guided by your Holy Spirit in just and equitable ways. Guide them, too, we pray, when they are aware and afraid of the power they wield.

Within the world, many are feeling isolated and alone, each day one to be faced with resignation, that this is another day to be got through, somehow. May the love of Jesus touch their hearts, so that they discover that they are not truly alone, and may we all be aware of one another, of those for whom a phone call, a friendly word will make their day special.

Within the world, too, many greet each day with joy, comfortable in their own skins. Thank you that we have a capacity to find happiness within the small and inconsequential. May we draw upon that skill to enhance our own and the lives of others, that Jesus' words, his promise of full life, may be a reality for all and everyone.

We ask it in his name.
Amen

Sounds around us

Boom twang cheep clatter bong whisper chatter squeak sing buzz roar rattle bang shout ...

Shhhh. . . .

Shh! What can you hear? For those who live near main roads, the diminution of traffic noise during Lockdown has been a blessing. The quiet has been appreciated, but traffic noise is not all that has been silenced. Church bells have mostly been silenced too.

In the seventies and eighties I was a keen bellringer here in the north east, then became an occasional one in Manchester and later at Swillington near Leeds. Ministry kind of largely crowded it out.

Why bellringing? Partly, it's all-absorbing. The kind of bellringing I'm talking about is Change Ringing, whereby you learn mathematical patterns (methods), the bells changing the position in which they strike at each stroke. Some of these are simple, others very complex, and when you're ringing, the concentration pushes all your worries aside. Not only do you have the pattern to remember, you might have a bell that has peculiar quirks of its own, and you have to think of your 'striking': the gap between each bell should be the same so that the rhythm is as near perfect as you can get. And then each bell has a wheel of a different diameter, which means it takes the deep bells longer to turn than the lighter ones, and that must be taken into account. I used to love ringing the smallest bell – the Treble – at Newcastle Cathedral, because of the skill needed to accommodate the far larger 10th, 11th and 12th bells. Very satisfying when you got it right!

Bellringing depends upon cooperation between the ringers and when it works well, the sense of collective endeavour and achievement, the being part of the creation of a harmonious sound is wonderful, maybe a similar feeing to singing in a choir. Making a joyful noise.

In the 1970s, I belonged to St. John's, Newcastle, ringing there too. On Easter Eve, there was (still is) a Vigil service at which the lighted Paschal candle is brought into the dark church, Christ's rising proclaimed and then the individual candles held by each are lit, the light slowly spreading around the building. Then all is light and glorious sound, and at the end of the service, we ringers rushed up to ring the bells, silenced since Maundy Thursday, so that the people leaving the church did so to the sound of rejoicing. I always found it profoundly moving.

We have been living through a very shadowy, largely silent time, unable to meet and join in creative enterprises, though technology has helped us draw together, albeit on screen. Easter will be with us almost unnoticed – what can we do and say and be: how do we rejoice?

Whatever our own feelings, the light of Christ has been moving quietly among us still, and maybe we needed that time apart to reflect on Christ with us, within us, holding us together in the silent times. The Psalmist asked, "How can we sing the Lord's song in a strange land?" (Psalm 137) How did we sing the Lord's song when it was noisy, when the pace of life itself, the noise and bustle, seemed to oppose us? How will we sing the Lord's song soon – in a new, joyful way?

The first verse of the "Bellringers Hymn", much of it applicable to us all!

> Unchanging God, who livest
> Enthroned in realms on high,
> To all the power thou givest
> Thy name to magnify.
> We raise the bells for ringing
> With ready mind and will,
> And come before thee, bringing
> Our hearts, our strength, our skill.
> Henry Charles Wilder, 1904 (altered, 'men' to 'all'!)

Ringers work together to make a joyful sound. We work together to be light in the world. Joyfully!

A prayer:

"The light shines in the darkness, and the darkness did not overcome it."
(John 1:5)

In the noise and bustle of the city street or the seaside town in summer, living Lord, you are there. In among the noise and fumes of the motorway, living Lord, you are there. In the quiet of the countryside and the stillness of the dawn, living Lord, you are there. In the sometimes oppressive silence in which many dwell, living Lord, you are there.

Unseen, unknown by many, fearless in the darkness, living Lord, your light, tremulous as we hold it, shines in our hearts. Draw us together, we pray. Uphold us, strengthen us, always that we might shine with your light for the world around us.

So much has been silenced, Lord, in this last year. Bells ringing out, the voices of children playing. We thank you for the ways we have discovered of sharing faith during this time, and for the possibilities that the future will bring.

So much has been silenced, yet so many voices have been heard. We pray for those who work within the media, to which many turn for comfort, to lose themselves. We pray the Holy Spirit's wisdom and discernment to guide their decisions and words, and the same for those who listen and view.

Loving Lord, when we are able to worship together again, may we bring our hearts, our strength, our skill in your service and may our voices ring with joy, the joy of knowing Christ, your Son, our Lord, in whose name we make our prayer.

Amen

One Whole Year!

The first Lockdown started a year ago. Also a year ago I began to produce these posters and Thoughts and Prayers while church services were suspended, imagining this was a task that might last a few weeks – and here we are 52 editions later! There were three churches on my list when I set out, but since then it has grown and grown, way beyond anything I could have imagined. I think the truth of the matter is that I had the right idea at the right time and it fulfilled, and fulfils still, a particular need.

This question of the 'right time' is one that crops up quite often in the Bible and is particularly pertinent as we approach Holy Week. Matthew tells us that when Jesus sent his disciples to prepare their Passover meal, he told them to tell the man they would meet, "The Teacher says, 'My time is near, I will keep the Passover at your house with my disciples'" (Matthew 26:18), and later, in the Garden of Gethsemane, "See, the hour is at hand when the Son of Man is betrayed into the hands of sinners" (Matthew 26:45). All came together at that moment.

The concept of Jesus' whole coming and ministry and death being at 'the right time' can be read: Jesus said, at the outset of his ministry, "The time is fulfilled, and the kingdom of God has come near; repent, and believe in the good news" (Mark1:15), and then Paul says, "But when the fullness of time had come, God sent his Son, born of a woman, born under the law,"

(Galatians 4:4). Surely there's something very reassuring about this, that things happen in their right time.

But there is also a warning:

"So when they had come together, they asked him, "Lord, is this the time when you will restore the kingdom to Israel? He replied, "It is not for you to know the times or periods that the Father has set by his own authority"
(Acts 1:6-7).

Now there's the snag. We like to have things planned out; you can see it in the way that the media is constantly asking questions that begin "When?" When will Lockdown be lifted, when can we go on holiday, when, when, when. And there can be no firm answer. Life – in my experience at least – has a chaotic edge to it and viruses in particular don't bother about the clock.

So how do we know when the right time comes for anything? If we try to use the Bible as Old Moore's Almanac, trying to discern times and futures in ancient prophesies we'll be doomed to disappointment. Jesus told us clearly, "It is not for you to know."

But what we are to do is discern the right moments. Jesus, after speaking the above words, went on to say to the disciples, "But you will receive power when the Holy Spirit has come upon you." (Acts 1:8). The Spirit will guide, as we remain open to that guidance, a guidance that we often notice only after the event. When these Thoughts began back on 29th March 2020, when Lockdown One prevented the celebration of the 5th anniversary of the redevelopment of Jesmond URC building, I wasn't consciously seeking the guidance of the Holy Spirit, but the Spirit guided, undoubtedly, and my own particular quirk of being able to see connections between the strangest of situations came to the fore. Of course, the thing is also to discern the right time to stop . . . !

These Thoughts go out over a wide area. I send to church contacts from Leeds in the South to Berwick in the north and to friends in Wolverhampton, Harrogate, Cumbria. I'm aware that they go much further as folk send them on to their friends, and I'm curious to know just how far they do travel. If you could send me some feedback on this, I'd be grateful, also to know if you're putting them on your church website – I do know of some, but probably not all.

The responses received revealed that they travel west as far as Rhyl, north as far as Edinburgh, south as far as Guernsey. Beyond Great Britain, they travel to Germany, Nigeria and South Africa. And, as people pass them on again, maybe further!

A prayer:

Living God, you are beyond all time yet reach into our time-constrained lives though the life, death and resurrection of Jesus, your Son, our Saviour.

We come before you in thanksgiving for each day, for each moment. We praise and bless you for the good moments of this past year, the quietness that has made us able to appreciate the birdsong, the buzz of insects, the sound of the wind rustling the leaves of the trees, the moments we have been able to think, quietly, of your blessings to us.

But we think, too, of the hard times, the restrictions that have sometimes seemed so burdensome, especially lately; the inability to visit and hold in our arms family, close friends; the losses many have suffered in people who have died, jobs that are gone; and we lay all this before you with aching hearts.

By your Spirit, bring comfort and peace, we pray. Some people have lost much. We pause and remember them. Some people have given much. We pause and remember them. Time rolls on, and we have no control over it, but we can seize the moment to do something good and positive.

Lord, guide us in wisdom we pray. By your Spirit, we ask that you guide those who have great decisions to make, especially regarding the Pandemic, that we may all be led through to rich and caring lives.

As Palm Sunday and Holy Week approach, we ask your blessing on our thinking and remembering. Help us enter into that particular time, to welcome Jesus with joy and with awe as he faces the trial and pain that must come before our Salvation is assured. Indeed, blessed is he who comes in the name of the Lord! Hosanna! Hosanna!

Amen

Christ is Risen!

Here we are celebrating Easter again, still in the midst of the Lockdown – did we even dream we'd be in this position a year ago? But we are encouraged to be hopeful, to rejoice even, as Lockdown is gradually eased and as more and more people are vaccinated: "Back to the life we love," says one headline.

But as I talk to my friends and neighbours, I find that many of us are distinctly nervous about resuming the life we had. I've always enjoyed driving, but now I find myself hesitant to tackle even quite a small journey, one that I wouldn't have thought twice about a year or so ago, and this even though I've probably been driving more than many people recently. (Mostly hospital visits! Great thing, age.) Now, when an enthusiastic shopaholic tells me she has no desire to go on a shopping binge, and when several people agree that the thought of going into a big supermarket makes them feel a bit sick, I can't help but feel that something has happened to us. In many ways the long periods of Lockdown, especially for those deemed vulnerable, has deskilled us and some of that may be good, in that we've learned to live more simply, but some is not good. No doubt in time things will normalise, but for now, many people are fearful.

Not very Easter-ish? Easter is a time of massive celebration, as we rejoice that Jesus rose from the dead and, with the disciples, we stand in awe and wonder at this great sign of the love of God: death itself, the final barrier, the final fear, is defeated.

But as we turn to the Gospel accounts of the resurrection, we find a great deal of fear. The women run from the tomb, terrified, even though they'd been told by an angel – surely a reliable source of information - that Jesus was risen (Mark 16:1-8, Luke 24:1-11). When Peter and another disciple run to the tomb, the other disciple gets there first but hesitates to go in and check (John 20:1-5). And in the evening, when you'd expect the disciples to be excited or at least hopeful, they're hiding away behind locked doors (John 20:19).

I don't think we should blame them or ourselves too much. All change is worrying, and the disciples were facing a massive change that challenged all their thinking. Were the women right in what they said? And if so, what would happen next? Their dreams and plans must have been totally wrecked, and 'what next' was shrouded in mystery, so it's no wonder they were scared. So huge a thing had happened that - I think I'd be scared too.

Joy came later, as Jesus came to them and it was then that they lost their fear in receiving his gift of the Holy Spirit, but it all took time and maybe they, like us, wanted the joy and certainty to come quickly. It will take us time not only to emerge from the fears we have, but it will also take time to process the changes to our lives and find joy in all that is to come. We have the knowledge of Jesus' rising, and whatever may be happening, nothing can take that away from us. However, if you're like me (you poor soul!) it can be hard to hold to that truth when life is strange. Just pause now. Let it sink in. God loves the world so much that new, eternal life is ours, this moment.

Perhaps one verse of my favourite Easter hymns might help us all - ' the green blade riseth, from the buried grain.'

> 'When our hearts are wintry, grieving, or in pain,
> then thy touch can call us back to life again,
> fields of our hearts that dead and bare have been:
> Love is come again, like wheat that springs up green.'
> John Macleod Campbell Crum (1872-1958)

A prayer:

In the cold of Golgotha, the disciples watched Jesus die, the man they had followed, loved, and who loved them with all their faults and weaknesses.

Then, in the cold of daybreak, the bright shining of new life came forth. To wintry hearts, afraid, lost, their hopes and plans in pieces around them, new life was offered. In the cold of daybreak, this gift seemed too incredible: Jesus, was risen from dead, the trappings of death laid aside. How could this be?

Eternal Lord God and Father, we sometimes find it incredible that Jesus died, rose again, for us. We have done nothing to deserve that love and the thought can terrify us, as it terrified them millennia ago.

Yet we rejoice, joyfully, wonderfully, for it is true: like the plant bursting from the earth's darkness to vibrant, beautiful life, Christ breaks the bonds of death, the bonds of fear.

We rejoice that, fearful and hesitant as we are, this new life is offered to us, each day. We rejoice, too, at the gift of new life seen all around us: new shoots breaking through the soil, the joyful colours of spring flowers, new hope breaking through tired lives.

Loving Lord, in a world where there seems so much darkness, bring your Easter light. In a world that is cold for so many, bring your Easter warmth. In a world where there is so much death – physical death and death of hope – bring your new life. For that life we praise and bless you, Father, Son and Spirit, today and always.

Amen

Low Sunday

Low Sunday is the name traditionally given to the Sunday after Easter; it's thought the name derives from the contrast between this Sunday and the High Festival of Easter. Jokingly, ministers often reckon it got the name because congregation sizes are low, people deciding that they deserve a Sunday off after Easter, and it is true, numbers are indeed lower and often ministers take the week as part of their annual holiday allowance. It will be interesting to see if Zoom attendance is down. Come on, folks: you're just in your own living room (or study or wherever), you don't even have to leave the house! And the non-essential shops aren't open yet.

But there is another meaning of low, one I have an uneasy feeling people might start to experience when restrictions are fully lifted.

We have longed and longed for the end to the Lockdown, the end of restrictions. We long to be able to meet up fully indoors, to hug, to go away on holiday, maybe to get back to work. We long for life to return to the way it was before, but the reality is that it's a long time since we've been able to do all of this and more, and things will have changed. People have died or moved away, we might find that our own outlook, or the outlook of family and friends, will have changed. I'm not being a prophet

of doom, just realistic, and we all know how things we really, really look forward to can be an anti-climax because we've laid so many expectations on them.

There has been a lot said about mental health during this time of Lockdown, and rightly so, but in this interim place we will need to be attentive to our own mental and emotional needs.

Research has shown that stroking a cat or dog has a particularly soothing effect, but then cats can be pretty relaxed. I remember years ago when I was running a Bible study in my house, two folk ended up, each with a cat on their knee (not the same cats as I have now) and these two people opened up remarkably as they stroked them. It was remarkable, because one of the people didn't usually share how she felt at all, and she commented afterwards on how surprisingly soothing it had felt just to stroke the cat. Now even the most well-behaved cat can be a bit of a nuisance sometimes, but I am now finding that when one hops on my knee and I consciously allow myself to take time to stroke it rather than pushing it off, I'm aware that my mood lifts. The cat's happy too, and purrs, and that also helps – the rumbling purr does create a sense of wellbeing. This is not a suggestion that you get yourself a cat or dog or guineapig or whatever; but finding what lifts your spirit and pursuing it is essential to our overall health.

When Jesus' disciples were in a very low place on the evening of the Resurrection, he came to them and said, "Peace be with you." and "As the Father has sent me, so I send you." (John 20:19-22) When he had said this, he breathed on them and said to them, "Receive the Holy Spirit" . They were given the comfort and the help they needed to get through the next few, strange weeks.

We are people of faith, but we are also human, with all our human

weaknesses and ups and downs: let's pray for the peace Jesus brings to fill our lives – and take steps to help that peace take root!

My garden helps me: gardening makes a massive difference to how I feel. I don't have a large garden, but it's surprising how much you can do with a little. Then there's a quiet service I try to get to each week that really lifts me up. And then there's reading, and there's writing – I get lost in that, but if I'm in a very low mood, my creativity heads for the hills. Like I said, we're human!

But these are my things - what are yours? Do you consciously cultivate what lifts your mood, makes you receptive to receiving Jesus' gift of peace? If not, why not?

A prayer:

"Peace be with you." These are beautiful words, words given us through the love of Jesus, through the love of the Father who sent him. They are beautiful words, loving Father, but when we try to grasp hold of them, they so easily slip away. Peace of heart seems elusive. Peace of the world, in hiding.

And we confess that our reaching out for peace can be half-hearted. We want it – we want it so much - but we also want to hold onto our resentments, our petty irritations, our foreboding. In the world, we want peace, but we also want power, and we cannot hold onto both. At this present moment, we want a resumption of normality, but we are afraid.

"Peace be with you," Jesus said, without laying down caveats, conditions. Forgive our hesitant grasping of that peace. At this time of great unease in the world, we earnestly pray peace.
* peace within hospitals, surgeries, care homes,
* peace in families where there is none,
* peace within nations where there is unrest and suspicion,
* peace between nations, where there is lust for power and dominion,
* peace in the church,
* peace in each heart.

We pray peace and healing for those who are ill, thinking especially today of those who are clinically depressed or who find themselves temporarily in a low place. We pray, too, the strength and guidance of the Holy Spirit for those who live with them and help them.

Loving God, in the days to come we will find many changes, some that we look forward to and others that we doubt. We pray the wisdom of the Holy Spirit in all the decisions that will be made, both collectively and in individual lives, that we may indeed have true confidence and peace as we move forward.

In Jesus' name we ask it.

Amen

The Call of Duty

Perhaps inevitably, this week's thoughts are influenced by the death of HRH Prince Philip, Duke of Edinburgh.

In the past couple of days we have heard often of his strong sense of duty, his putting aside of his own career in total commitment to supporting and working with the Queen. It showed in great and small ways: I remember watching them descending from the carriage that took them to the Opening of Parliament at a time when neither were well, and the way in which he was alert, watching the Queen, a hand ready to steady her if she stumbled.

Duty. It's a strange word that can have a negative connotation – 'You're only doing this because you think it's your duty.' And duty does have a tough side; there are tasks we'd rather not be doing but feel it's our duty to do, and we go reluctantly: I suspect that all but the saints among us feel that way sometimes, and I'm sure the Royal Family does too. But we – and they - go.

The positive aspect of duty refers to our duty to care for those about us, or at least to have a concern for them. Jesus called us along this pathway of caring for our neighbour (Luke 10: 27), but there is a subtlety to it that we need to note. We are called to care for others, not dominate them with our ideas of what they need. I love the quote from C.S. Lewis' The Screwtape Letters, "She's the sort of woman who lives for others and you can tell the others by their hunted expression." Prince Philip's tremendous legacy of The Duke of Edinburgh Award is the antithesis of this, a scheme whereby young people can find their own strengths, learn to cope with difficulty and to get along with others, not through compulsion, but because they want to. Then there is his work with the Alliance of Religions and Conservation (ARC), a manifestation of care for the whole of creation and of the faith he and we bring to all our tasks.

Commitment: that quality of seeing a task through, even when things go wrong and people grumble at you. Not easy. Even that person profoundly committed to the task, St Paul, got frustrated on occasion, as when he lost his côol with Corinthian criticism, "Do we not have the right to be accompanied by a believing wife, as do the other apostles? Is it only Barnabas and I who have no right to refrain from working for a living?" (1 Corinthians 9:3-11). He sounds tired and fed up.

Maybe there's something in knowing yourself and thinking through what really matters, and working and praying through what our faith may require us to commit to, and what our faith teaches us about being fully ourselves. I think in this regard, Prince Philip is a good model, because he seems to have found things that mattered to him, personally, and to work with and on them, alongside the duty tasks. Finding what gives us strength and doing it makes the duty side of life that bit easier to cope with.

We give thanks for a life well lived, one that has affected very many lives and will, I suspect, continue to do so. May we be guided as we carry out the duties laid upon us to find the joy and release that God also wills for us.

I had the privilege of shaking hands with the Queen and Prince Philip in 2012, at an event in Buckingham Palace to mark the 200th anniversary of

the birth of Charles Dickens, to which people with a connection through academia or the arts (I was there through the Dickens Fellowship) were invited. Rather more deservingly, I was presented to Princess Anne years ago at an AGM of the Save the Children Fund of which she is President, for my part in re-establishing a branch of SCF in Amble. I am no Royalist (a definite Cromwellian!) but on both these occasions I was impressed and touched by the presence and commitment of these very gracious people.

Whether a life is lived well in the public eye, or quietly, just you where you are, that life is valuable. Find peace, in who you are.

A prayer:

Living God, who holds all within your eternal care, we rejoice that you offer to each the strength to be the people you need us to be, the people we long to be.

We rejoice too in knowing Jesus, who gave his life to the uttermost to bring healing and peace and ultimately new, eternal life so that death, our final unknown, need no longer be feared.

At this time of national mourning, we pray for all who mourn loved ones who have died, and those who mourn loved ones who are missing or separated because of quarrels, misunderstandings, or for no apparent reason. We pray healing. We pray peace.

As the national focus falls upon the Duke of Edinburgh Award Scheme, we pray for young people everywhere, and especially those who are facing obstacles to progress, whatever these may be; those who have little or no confidence in themselves or those who have potential to give much to the world but lack the backing of influential adults. We pray your guiding, encouraging Spirit to bring both confidence and a sense of reality, that they may find their own true pathway, and in that pathway, a real joy.

We pray for ourselves that, encouraged by the example of those who have gone before us and for the sake of those who follow on, we may accept gladly those tasks that you need us to fulfil for the growth of your Kingdom of justice and peace.

We ask it in the name of Jesus who gave his life that all may have life in all its fullness.
Amen

Knowing One Another

Guess who? No, not the dog, silly!

Watching the funeral of the Duke of Edinburgh, I was struck by the music he had commissioned and the readings he had chosen; it gave me insight into the person of a very public figure, and that prompted the thought: how often we hear people say after a funeral, "I never knew that about them!" It's a mark of a good funeral that it reflects the person as they really were, and that is conveyed through the style of the whole, as well as what is said.

Thinking on all this, I reflected on the current obsession with knowing our distant ancestors – DNA tests to see if we're related to Angles, Saxons, Vikings, Romans et al. And I reflected on the sadness that people spend time and money on this, yet often know very little about the early lives of their own parents or grandparents and I wondered how this had come about. When I was teaching in the seventies and early eighties, I found that children were very interested in 'the olden days' and hearing how things were different or the same when I was a child. I remember one girl bringing in a "Bunty" comic and being highly surprised that I'd had it when I was her age – and both of us being disgusted to find one serial still running! I know recycling is good, but really!

As a child, I was regaled with stories from my parents' youth, and occasionally my grandparents would tell a colourful tale or two, but I was quite a withdrawn child who also listened in a lot and probably heard more than I was supposed to and learned a lot about people. But, thinking back, I remember that television didn't have the hold it gained later: our family got a television for the Coronation, but there was only BBC and it had limited hours anyway. We talked, and I suspect the difference between then and now lies partly in that.

But it's sad, when you think how often we only find out interesting things about people from their funerals. Why don't we engage with them while they're alive and we could ask questions? Valuing the living while they're around? How many of you, like me, have found that when you move on from an employment you're told how much you've been appreciated and how sad it is you're going and you think to yourself, "If you'd said all of this before, I wouldn't have handed in my notice."

How much are we genuinely interested in the lives of the people around us? Do we let people know they're valued for who they are? One of the things said about the Pandemic is that it's helped people get to know their neighbours, instead of them being as ships that pass in the night; an interesting point, that restrictions and distancing have actually helped people grow closer. Will that interest continue? I hope so, for all our sakes.

If we look at St Paul's letters, we find, usually at the beginning or end, personal notes. In Romans 16:1-15, he commends a deacon of the church, Phoebe, asking that they give her all the help she needs; he praises Prisca and Aquila for risking their necks for him, and speaks of many, many more. These are people he knew and cared about, even when he was having a tough time himself. And all these he mentions would have known and understood him. They wouldn't have had to wait for his funeral in order to find out about him!

Jesus' disciples had the gift of his resurrected presence with them for a time: we don't have that luxury. Let's value and learn from one another, now.

Research has shown that trees 'communicate' with each other through their roots underground. Many aspects of nature involve creatures understanding each other and the plant life around them – I wonder why we humans, with our greater brains, can't manage this communication stuff so well?

A prayer:

Trees stand quiet, serene, each a home and feeding place for so many creatures, great and small. Bees and flies buzz by, busy, involved in their own lives but understanding the plants on which they feed, the earth in which they live.

And we walk or watch, sometimes aware of our connection to it all, but so often heedless, involved in our own thoughts, our own busyness.

Creator God, you who hold all within your great care, open our eyes, ears and minds to the world about us, to the people around us. Help us to hear and to understand. "O Lord, how manifold are your works! In wisdom you have made them all. When you take away their breath, they die and return to their dust. When you send forth your spirit, they are created; and you renew the face of the ground." (Psalm 104:24a,29-30)
Help us to hear and to understand.

We bring with thanksgiving those who are no longer with us upon earth, those whom we have known and those of whom we have heard. We thank you for all in their lives that spoke of your care, for the blessing they were and the continued blessing of the memories they leave behind, the work they began that others continue.

And we pray for those who mourn, that they might not do so as people without hope. Bring your peace to troubled hearts, we pray, and help us listen with open minds to those things they want to share with us. Help us to hear and to understand.

Loving Lord, speak to us. By your Spirit, guide us in all our doings and in all our interaction with others and with you. Help us to hear and to understand.

Our prayers we offer in the name of Jesus your Son our Saviour.
Amen

Escape to the Seaside

Having had a rather difficult morning on Friday (understatement) I longed to go to Seaham, a coastal town about fifteen miles away. I hadn't seen the sea for over a year, having obeyed the injunction to stay local, but could bear the loss no longer, so set out. It was a beautiful, sunny day and I couldn't but compare it with the first time I visited: I'd been in Durham some months, and on my day off decided to try this place Seaham. It was a very windy day (another understatement – gale-force winds) and as I struggled to open the car door against the wind I thought, "Is this wise?" Probably not: the wind was vicious and the sea grey and turbulent, the surface dotted with little mounds of foam, but these caught and dispersed the sun's rays to create scores of rainbow clumps against the grey. The sight was unique. A perhaps unwise trip that proved wonderful.

This Friday, the sea was blue and the wind gentle. As I walked, I thought of all the good visits I'd had there over the years, my dog haring along the beach; I also thought back to when I lived in Amble, in what remains my favourite house of the many in which I've lived. It was a sturdy stone-built terrace so near the sea that I could hear the waves crashing against the sea-wall or, on calmer nights, be soothed by the gentle rattle of the shingle as the sea ebbed and flowed. I stood for ages listening to just that sound on Friday, watching the wavelets come and go and letting my thoughts come and go with them.

In the Bible, the sea is synonymous with chaos, a dangerous place to a desert-dwelling people and indeed, you don't mess with the sea. There's that lovely passage in Psalm 107 verses 23-32, the vivid description of those who "went down to the sea in ships" and the perils they faced – and that God brought them "to their desired haven." Only God could understand and control the sea: Job 38: 4-11 is a beautiful expression of this view, look at the connection in that passage of the sea with the clouds and with darkness. How often are we aware of the connections within creation? Can we make ourselves more aware?

As I stood watching the sea in its tranquil mode, I reflected on the way that it works its own work, one that connects with the whole earth and beyond. I remembered one night in Amble, lying awake in bed as the wind howled, rattling its way down the street, and then, as if someone had switched a switch, the wind was stilled in an instant. The tide had turned. It was remarkable. Then I reflected on the way that the sea rearranges the adaptive earth, removing parts here, adding them there. Earth, sea, cosmos, all connecting. I find it very comforting to be aware of being a tiny part of that great evolving life, all of which is held in the love of God.

At this time, when we have been largely isolated and when there seems so much that divides us, remembering our oneness with creation is good; on a practical level, it makes us aware of our own effect on all around us, but it can also balance those tensions we feel, remind us that we are part of something much greater and always held lovingly by God, Father, Son and Spirit.

With those who go down to the sea in ships and with the Elders in John's vision of the Throne of God, before which lies the sea (Revelation 4: 1-11), we offer our praise and joy, now and always.

Seaham was a mining town with three collieries and was also a port for export of coal, but of late years it has been turned around: the beach is clean, the rockpools home to sea anemones and crabs and probably much else (I confess I'm not keen on little things that live in shells!). Plus, the geology of the place is fascinating.

I love the great variety of the pebbles and the way they have been smoothed over so many years by the action of the sea, to and fro.

Like the pebbles, our rough edges can be smoothed by life shaking us about, but at all stages we are loved and valued by God, whether we gleam like diamonds or are a rather dull muddy colour. We all have a place and a role.

A prayer:

Calling upon the name of Jesus, we come before you, Living God and Father; reaching towards you, we long to follow the way of Christ in humility and joy.

Eternal God, who holds all within your great love, we praise you. Always watching over your creation, you guide us through your Spirit, teaching us how to live in harmony with your will in all our doings. In our lives, Lord, we confess that we do not always behave or speak as we should or even how we want to do, yet we remember the assurance that nothing can separate us from your love in Jesus Christ.

Trusting in your love, we bring our prayer
for those who suffer in this world.

* those who suffer flood, watching their
homes and livelihood disappear,
* those who suffer crop failure again and again,
who face starvation,
* those who suffer deeply through lack
of medical equipment, through poverty,
* those who live within repressive regimes,
rights and liberties curtailed,
* those who are imprisoned on account of their faith
or for standing up for the poor and marginalised,
* those who have lost family and friends and those who mourn,
* those who are afraid.

And we pray for those who are seeking to make a difference in
this world.
* those who work in poverty-stricken areas,
* those who bring aid where there is hunger, sickness and loss,
* those who bring aid into violent places, helping those
caught between warring factions,
* those who work in refugee camps and centres,
* those who speak out boldly against injustice.

Loving Lord, as we reflect on the turbulence of the world, we
cannot see a way of peace. Show us, we pray, the rainbows
amongst the brooding greyness, those signs of hope and joy.

We ask it in the name of Jesus, who brings life in all its fullness.
Amen

Words WORDS Words WORDS WORDS *Words*

I wonder how many words we hear and speak in an average lifetime? Certainly more than we would have been using a few centuries ago when quietness surrounded the greater part of life, days before television or even radio came to be constantly wittering away in the background. I admit this is so in my own home much of the time. If we add to the mix the words we use inside our own heads as we think, the number would shoot up in both past and present times.

Something that has always fascinated me when I watch toddlers playing alone is how they, pre-language, are thinking, because thinking they clearly are. Also interesting is the fact that children understand what is being said long before they can speak – it's true, so be careful what you say!

Be careful what you say. A rubric that applies to our ordinary lives certainly applies with force to those who are famous or in possession of great power as we see almost every day when we open our newspapers or check out the news on radio or television. Accusations – "You said . . . " Denials. Counter accusations of deceit and sleaze, some deserved, some not.

The difficulty with words, of course is that they can be misheard, misunderstood and misinterpreted, even on a trivial level. I remember when I was in Manchester, someone spoke of a church member who had been suffering for years with Parkinson's Disease and was terribly thin. "And she was such a bonny woman," she said sadly. "I think she still looks pretty," I said, an observation greeted with A Strange Look. It was only later I discovered that 'bonny' there meant 'plump' rather than generally attractive, as I understood the word. Ho Hum. You live and learn and along the way some of your church members suspect you're a bit odd, but this is only solved by using more words to start to understand one another.

None of this is new. There are warnings within the Old Testament - "Your wealthy are full of violence; your inhabitants speak lies, with tongues of deceit in their mouths." (Micah 6:12) and when we turn to the New Testament, there is a whole section in the letter of James on the subject of "taming the tongue" in Chapter 3, verses 1-12. We can recognise much within it. "From the same mouth come blessing and cursing." True, is it not?

We would like to think that good words, blessings fall from our mouths, but unless we're perfect, other words sneak through. Weasel-words that seek to please. Little lies. A bit of gossip. The damaging half-truths.

But it's hard, isn't it, finding that balance between a censorious attitude and one in which anything goes? Hard to know our own motivation. I don't know about you, but through the years I have become nervous of people who begin what you know will be criticism with the words, "I'm saying this in Christian love . . . " I'd much rather they began with, "Look, you're not going to like me for this but . . . " Honesty. When I was at Grammar School, a friend of one of my friends was someone I really disliked, until one day she said to me, "I don't like you," and I replied, "I don't like you either," and we got on pretty well after that! A true story.

Detail from window depicting the Crucifixion, Jesmond United Reformed Church

I doubt the day will come when there is that kind of honesty in governments or in other bastions of power (and even in the Church?); there will be half-truths, and evasion and, among the populace, rumour and gossip. Pray that we see and navigate our way through all this and let our own tongues speak with honesty and compassion. It might change the world!

Words can hurt and words can heal, and quietness bring peace.

Words build us up or pull us down. We might be able to mind our language when speaking to others, but how many of us say harsh words to ourselves, either out loud or in our heads? Those words carry great power to weaken us, make us less capable of facing the world. Jesus died that we need not carry that kind of shame. Forgiveness and new beginning are his gift to us.

A prayer:

Eternal, living Lord God our Father, reaching within our multiplicity of inadequate words, we speak and sing your praise. Jesus Christ, Son of God, Living Word before all words, we speak and sing your praise.
Holy Spirit, giver of words to speak and silence to keep, we speak and sing your praise.

In these times when we have been restricted in our meeting with others, thank you for the many ways we have found to communicate, to grow close, even to sing, through use of new and old media, of Zoom and letters, of simple wave and thank you as we pass by strangers and friends.

Help us, God who exists in perfect unity of communication, Father, Son and Spirit, to learn from the times we have had to discover new ways to reach out to others so that we might understand one another better.

Forgive us, we ask, when we prefer not to understand, but to condemn.

Thank you for the times we have had to remain silent, and for the times in our lives when the quiet presence of another has helped us cope and given us new strength to live anew.

Thank you especially for the knowledge of Christ's presence with us, and for the forgiveness and new life he brings.

Give to us, we pray, an openness – an openness of ears and minds to hear and understand those different to us, those we find it hard to like, and an openness to hear you speaking to us through the words of people, through all we see and receive in creation, through the deep quietness that indeed brings a healing of sore and bruised lives.

Help us rediscover your task for us, your word to us today. Loving Father, we pray for that day when true understanding will fill the earth, when boundaries will be broken down and words of gentleness and hope, not words of anger and despair, will fill the earth.

We ask it in the name of Jesus, the Living Word.
Amen

Filling a Vacuum

No, not a vacuum flask! I'm sure you all know the hazards in doing that. And sorry, I can't illustrate the other kind of vacuum, for obvious reasons . . .

The saying goes that nature abhors a vacuum, and if we look at the disciples met together between the Ascension of Jesus and Pentecost, we find them acting out that very adage.

Acts 1: 12-26. Returning to Jerusalem they gathered themselves together in "the room upstairs where they were staying" (v. 13), and got their heads together. Here they were, told to wait for the promise of the Father, but you know how it is – you have to do something, and they didn't know how long they'd have to wait anyway. Yes, they were praying, but surely there was something else . . . and perhaps inevitably it was Peter who stood up and suggested what that something could be. Drawing on Scripture, he argued that they should choose someone from among those who had been with Jesus from the beginning to take the place of Judas. They had no idea how the future was going to pan out, but they did know about the past: Jesus had called twelve of them, so the logical thing was to make that number back up, and they went about it in a time-honoured way. Two names were put forward, they all prayed and then drew lots, and the lot fell upon Matthias.

Good planning for the future, you could say, but look what they were actually doing - trying to plan the future on the basis of how the past had been. Twelve disciples then, twelve disciples now.

And what about poor Matthias, who I'm sure was a perfectly nice man, devoted to Jesus? From this point on we hear nothing more of him. On the other hand, we hear a great deal about the man God was going to choose in his own time – Saul of Tarsus – and in fact we are largely here because he accepted his calling.

Now the question, if you haven't guessed it already. As the Church restarts in a serious way, will we be like the disciples and try to force a pattern that pertained before the Pandemic struck?

I pose the question because we have moved through a completely new experience over the past year, which has affected us all. People we haven't seen since before the first Lockdown look different, sometimes older (well, we are!). We have learned new skills and let go of others. Maybe our priorities have changed; I know of several people who have revised their thinking on possessions and spending, others who find the natural world more significant. I'm sure you know of other changes there have been.

I think there's an important pattern in Acts to watch out for in our own life. The temptation to run ahead of God is massive and, like the disciples, those ideas we have can seem the absolutely right thing to do. But modern psychology warns us against making big decisions after a life-changing or traumatic event and this last year-and-a-bit has certainly been life-changing and in some cases even traumatic, so perhaps we should beware of that urge to do something quickly. Doing nothing is allowed! We need space to think, to pray.

Centuries ago, if there was a big decision to be made in the life of the nation, a national fast was declared to give people time to fast and pray in advance of the decision. Could it be that in the Church we need to allow time out to be together again and to pray, alone or with others, in an open, quiet, seeking way before we try to fit everything back together exactly as it was or try to turn everything on its head?

One of the new things I've just done is upgrade my mobile phone, and the quality of the camera is striking.

This is a Common Carder Bee feeding on Lungwort, and the detail certainly couldn't have been captured on my previous phone, good though it was.

Perhaps what we all need is a new lens through which to view the world more clearly as it now is, in our own lives and in the Church.

A prayer:

In an uncertain world, Loving Father, we seek your certainty. So much has been lost in the past year or so; there is so much we have missed, so much we have longed for and now a return to it all is tantalisingly close.

We want to run ahead, to grasp new possibilities – or do we actually want to turn back to things as they were pre-Lockdown?

Only you, Lord, truly know our hearts, only you understand the people we are, the people the past has formed us to be, has formed the ways we react. You, Lord, truly know our hearts – and in your Son, Jesus, you have offered us a glimpse of what we can be: people living with an openness to your guiding Spirit, people loving neighbours, finding joy in being together and joy in quiet solitude.

In this time of potential new beginning, help us follow Jesus more fully, ready to wait if that is what you need of us, and ready for action when you will.

As we rejoice in the number of vaccinations and reductions in the death rate, we pause to bring those who still suffer COVID-19 and its effects, thinking particularly of those countries where the rate of infection and death is still high, and where medical facilities are struggling.

Loving Father, bring healing and hope we pray, and may the strong help the weak across borders of ethnicity and faith. May the wisdom of the Spirit and the peace of Christ fill the corridors of power, and the minds and hearts of those who have great decisions to make, ones that will affect us all.

And may that same Spirit and peace fill the Church, that we might face with courage, hope and joy the challenges before us in the coming days.

These prayers we offer in the name of Jesus, your Son, our Saviour. Amen

Pentecost

This is the last of the 'Thoughts and Prayer' and associated posters. Ending what has been a way of life for 60 weeks was not an easy decision, but this truly seems to be the appropriate moment to stop. I began, all those weeks ago, on the 5th Anniversary of the redevelopment of Jesmond United Reformed Church and I'm going to end there.

The work was needed: Jesmond URC building was attractive but 'of its day' and in need of substantial adaptation to meet the needs of the present time. After long debate (years), a new plan was agreed. As their Pastoral Friend during ministerial vacancy, I chaired the Development Group.

The architect described the building as "a sleeping beauty" and indeed, the transformation was amazing.

The pillars were revealed in their beauty, lifting eyes and hearts, and the stained glass windows could be seen clearly. It was warm, both physically and in terms of the surprisingly intimate feel of what is a vast space. And a new entrance, created from the rather shabby area between church and halls is now a focus of real openness and welcome.

What has this to do with Pentecost? For me, it illustrates the encouraging aspect of the coming of the Holy Spirit. So often we think of the Spirit turning lives upside down, and while that does happen, more usually our allowing the Spirit to work within frees up that part of us that God sees: the inspiringly beautiful inside (yes, you too!). The Spirit enables us to be the people we were created to be. For Jesus' disciples, the coming of the Spirit at Pentecost brought them a new understanding and a new courage to speak out, to inspire others to believe, not only by their words but by who they were. (Read Acts 2: 1-42, a long passage, but worth a careful reading.)

Over the years we, like the church building, have been shaped in ways that were good at the time and suited the moment, but that maybe now mask aspects of ourselves that should be used anew. In the church, the raised dais was covered in carpet, hiding beneath which was a beautiful marble tile checker-board design that is now restored to its original loveliness. Are there gifts you have, hidden through the years, that need to be released in our post-Lockdown freedom? Will you let the Holy Spirit work with you in this?

One of the things that worried us about the redevelopment at Jesmond was the effect on the acoustic of the building, which was excellent; important because of the strong musical tradition of the church. Yet wonderfully, the acoustic was actually improved and music, secular and religious, rises gloriously. Again, if we let the Spirit free within us, the aspects of our lives that have been a blessing to us and to others won't be lost, but rather be enhanced.

This Pentecost, as we hopefully move towards a 'new normal', don't be afraid to ask that the Spirit works a gentle work of redevelopment in all our lives that will bring great blessing, today and in all the days to come. I pray that this will be so for you.

Why a picture of a table? This was created from the decorative front of the pews, with the table-top made of wood from the pews: plain, ordinary pine.

What has been in our lives – complicated, plain, even the seemingly left-over parts - can be reworked through the work of the Holy Spirit into something not only beautiful, but useful too!

A prayer:

At this Pentecost season we praise you, Living, Holy God, for the gift of the Holy Spirit, poured out upon the surprised disciples who were waiting, expectant, but not knowing the gift, the blessing that was to come to them.

We confess, Lord, that we are less expectant. In many ways, we feel we should be masters of our own destiny, are alright as we are, are used to being the people we have become through the years. The idea of letting the Holy Spirit work within our lives makes us nervous – we are afraid that our lives may be made uncomfortable, that you may ask of us more than we are able to give.

Yet we remember that you are a God of love, and that you know us, see us deep within. You know our weaknesses and you know, too, our hidden strengths and gifts, and understand all that has made us the people we are today.

But you also know the people we can be: by your Spirit, lead us into that state of being in which we are truly ourselves and truly a blessing to you and to others. This we pray.

And in our hurting world, we earnestly pray the blessing of your Spirit to bring wisdom to those in government at home and abroad as decisions are made about loosening restrictions, about travel, about world economy.

We pray, too, that same blessing in all areas where there is conflict and where there is domination of peoples by others, where there is injustice, we pray the Spirit's wisdom.

We pray especially for the current situation in Israel/Palestine, that peace and a just solution may come about.

Loving Lord, send your Spirit of gentleness anew, and may your Kingdom of justice and peace come for all people. Jesus showed us a way of living that builds up and does not destroy, that sees the saint in the sinner, that is costly, but brings peace.

May your Spirit form all our lives into that costly love, today and ever.

Amen

Thank you for sharing these thoughts and prayers,
which I pray will help you too in your lives.

I end as I always ended, week by week –
Blessings, Ruth

Registered Charity No. 701514

Profits from this book will go to Waddington Street Centre (WSC), which is a mental health charity based in Durham City. We will celebrate our 40th anniversary in November 2021 and as part of our celebrations we are trying to raise £40,000 so that we can purchase a new minibus.

We are a community committed to mutual support, kindness and hope. All of our members have mental health needs and WSC is a safe space where members, volunteers and staff work together to make recovery possible.

We are open 6 days per week and 4 evenings per week. Our week is jam packed with practical and emotional support, informal adult education, creative activities, sports activities, social gatherings and outings.

We believe in keeping people busy with interesting and enjoyable activities. Having positive distraction and a sense of purpose is necessary for everyone's mental health.

In addition, we offer supported accommodation for those at risk of homelessness. Our two shared houses and four single occupancy flats give our tenants a safe place to live and the opportunity to develop independent living skills. We also work with Durham's mental health hospital – Lanchester Road, to deliver support to those being discharged.

COVID-19 has really taken its toll on our members and they need our support more than ever. Sadly, we've had to reduce our services in the past year but have adapted to new ways of working and our daily telephone support has been greatly appreciated by many. Our members call us a 'lifeline'.

After this trying and difficult time, we really want our 40th anniversary to be a joyful and hopeful event. Sadly, we know that many more are struggling with their mental health as a result of the Pandemic. As such, we hope to continue our much-needed support for many years to come.

Ali Lee, Centre Manager

You can find out more by visiting **www.waddingtoncentre.co.uk**